Praise for *Essential*

"*To transform an organization, you must first transform its leaders.* Essential *shows the way forward for revolutionizing the way we work, through Smith and Monahan's innovative approach to human-powered leadership.*"

—**Angela Ahrendts DBE**,
former Apple SVP and Burberry CEO.

"Essential *provides a leadership roadmap that details how to harness the power of human intelligence in combination with AI to unleash true innovation and reach our fullest potential. This book provides a much-needed roadmap for unlocking and inspiring our workforces during this dynamic era.*"

—**Hayden Brown**,
CEO, Upwork

"Essential *offers a visionary roadmap for modern leadership, blending the latest in AI technology with a deeply human approach. Christie Smith and Kelly Monahan expertly guide leaders on how to create thriving, adaptable teams in an era of constant change.*"

—**Dorie Clark**,
Wall Street Journal bestselling author

ESSENTIAL

ESSENTIAL

How Distributed Teams,
Generative AI, and Global Shifts
Are Creating a New
Human-Powered Leadership

Christie Smith, PhD
Kelly Monahan, PhD

WILEY

Published by John Wiley & Sons, Inc., Hoboken, New Jersey.
Published simultaneously in Canada.

For general information on our other products and services or for technical support, please contact our Customer Care Department within the United States at (800) 762-2974, outside the United States at (317) 572-3993 or fax (317) 572-4002.

Wiley also publishes its books in a variety of electronic formats. Some content that appears in print may not be available in electronic formats. For more information about Wiley products, visit our web site at www.wiley.com.

Library of Congress Cataloging-in-Publication Data is Available:

ISBN: 9781394276585 (cloth)
ISBN: 9781394276592 (ePub)
ISBN: 9781394276608 (ePDF)

Cover Design: Wiley
Cover Image: © Ron Dale/Shutterstock
Author Photos: (Smith) photo by Olivia Steuer, (Monahan) photo by Kelly Monahan

SKY10091807_112224

*To all leaders – especially those
with the courage to embrace
our shared humanity.*

Contents

Introduction

As we write this book, we live in a world we'd describe as tense, uncertain, and increasingly polarized. It's at moments like these that we usually turn to leadership to guide us through the unknown and allay our fears. And yet today, trust in the institutions that have historically safeguarded our well-being and provided opportunity is at an all-time low. In place of hope, connection, and civility, what we see around us are overwhelming levels of disillusionment, disengagement, and division. Leadership is failing.

Our decades-long careers have been spent researching and consulting Fortune 500 companies and their C-suites on how to build thriving teams with a philosophy that when people do well, so does business. This approach to our work is in no small measure derived from our educational backgrounds in industrial psychology, organizational leadership, and clinical social work. Above all, we feel a responsibility and a drive to serve humanity – to improve the way we live by revolutionizing the way we work.

As a Baby Boomer and Millennial team, we have experienced the workforce differently, and yet share a strong conviction that the way we work, and thus lead, must change. As mentors and trusted colleagues, we bear witness to the level of confusion, burnout, anxiety, and frustration people experience in their jobs and this environment every day, even in our

1

youngest generation. We too are disappointed and angry – with leaders unwilling to relinquish power to invest in their only sure path to progress: people. It is from this position that we set forth to write this book, to inspire a new kind of leadership to meet the requirements and challenges of our evolving world.

Of course, the need for a new leadership paradigm born out of external crises is a historical pattern. When the Black Death wiped out as much as 60% of the world's population in the fourteenth century, medieval thinking about the human condition as one of necessary suffering transformed. The bleak, faceless feudal system gave way to capitalism, and politically the dominance of the Church was ultimately challenged by increasingly powerful states. A new philosophy, known as humanism, evolved to form the cornerstone of the Renaissance, perhaps the most revolutionary advance in Western civilization. Humanism introduced the idea that people were individuals, championed self-determination, and created an environment that supported rather than suppressed individual expression.

The Renaissance is just one example of how catastrophic disruptions can generate far-reaching social and economic change, often in surprising and even positive ways – at least in the long term. Most recently, of course, the daily reminders from natural and man-made disasters of our own mortality, along with inflation, political instability, environmental change, and widening disparities in the quality of life for minority communities, have similarly combined to awaken a new humanism enabled by new technologies that together seek another reinvention of society.

For businesses, a decade of disruption is transforming the nature of work. Leaders have been buffeted by relentless technological innovation, shifting demographics, and waves of economic shocks, including health crises, recession, inflation, global political instability, and supply chain interruptions. Social and cultural values increasingly play a major role in the brand image of all organizations, in the eyes of both customers and employees. And new technologies, like generative AI, are creating a wealth of new opportunities, but also overwhelming employees and leaders alike.

The impacts of these far-reaching changes have forced a global reimagination of what great leadership looks like in an uncertain world. Many leaders today still yearn for the top-down "good old days," when senior management was in control of their organizations and decision-making was relatively easy. But the solutions to today's challenges aren't found in the past. Regardless of now-constant economic shocks and waves of disruption, the long-term trajectory of uninterrupted business transformation requires a total reinvention of the very concept of leadership.

We've dedicated our careers to empowering and enabling companies to thrive through a human-powered approach to leadership. Our experience and research show that for businesses to thrive, so must their people. Over the last decade, we've witnessed:

- The growth rate of our labor force slow down
- A digital-everything world introduce new business and operating models
- The supply and demand of essential skills thrown off-balance, and in some cases, employees gaining the upper hand in where, when, and how much they work

COVID-19 and its aftermath accelerated these developments, but they did not begin with it, nor will they end with its resolution. Underlying the sudden shift to hybrid working models, the Great Resignation, quiet quitting, and other artifacts of COVID-19 were already potent and demonstrable shifts in population dynamics, skilling, and attitudes about labor and business. Even before the economic shocks of the last few years, the transformation of labor markets, flattening organizational models, and worker portability were leading us to a new understanding of employment. The pandemic only served to speed up the inevitable. These forces will continue to generate unanticipated disruptions for businesses and the global economy long after our current crises abate.

As the World Economic Forum reported in January 2023, millions of workers continue to leave their jobs every month, with some industries losing nearly 10% of their employees in the last 12 months alone. In the US, the independent workforce, or "freelancer" economy, grew from 40 million to 50 million workers between 2020 and 2021. Women in particular are voting with their feet, resigning from leadership positions in tech and other key industries in disproportionate numbers, taking with them, according to data from the Federal Reserve, over $1 trillion in economic value – more than half of what they have added since 1970.

Employees aren't simply leaving for better pay or the chance to work from home. According to the Pew Research Center, "lack of opportunities for advancement" and "feeling disrespected at work" were among the top reasons Americans quit their jobs in 2021. The survey also finds that those who quit and who are now employed elsewhere are more likely than not to say their current job has better pay, more opportunities for advancement, and more work–life balance and flexibility. Put simply, workers now expect considerable autonomy when it comes to the conditions of their employment.

Beyond rapid turnover and a shift to self-employment, stakeholder discontent is also manifesting itself more in the form of legal change. Even companies such as Amazon, Starbucks, Apple, and Google, long considered worker paradises, are facing growing unionization efforts. In Europe and in some US states, legislation requiring board representation that more closely reflects gender and racial demographics is forcing dramatic realignments. Salary transparency and disparity reporting is being mandated in much of the world.

Meanwhile, antitrust authorities worldwide have declared war on business consolidation, blocking mergers in every industry in hopes of reducing concentration and reigniting competition in the interests of consumers, employees, investors, and suppliers – embracing the core idea of "stakeholder value." What we are experiencing is nothing short of a stakeholder uprising. Business leaders must adapt, and adapt quickly, to new ways of thinking, collaborating, and working in general. Adapt, or become irrelevant.

Demands on CEOs – and others in the C-suite, boards of directors, and rising business leaders – to face these challenges have increased dramatically. A new way of managing is desperately required, one that rejects much of the conventional and outdated wisdom of the last 50 years. Every leader, every business, and every industry must transform – and quickly – to reinvent themselves as flexible, human-driven enterprises if they are to flourish into the future.

We're facing the most significant management crisis we've seen in decades of working one-on-one with senior executives. So far, business leaders have largely followed, rather than taken the lead, in operationalizing the new reality of work. Most are dangerously lagging, threatening the long-term sustainability of their organizations. And while our research shows that most executives understand the necessity of transformative change, few have taken even the first baby steps toward leading in an increasingly stakeholder-driven economy – one in which employ-ees, customers, suppliers, investors, and regulators compete to set the terms of business for organizations of all sizes.

In large part, that's because today's leaders simply don't know where to begin. A 2023 "Work Innovators" survey from the Upwork Research Institute finds that the majority of leaders (55%) are doubling down on their existing operating and talent strategies or seeking greater efficiencies within them. Yet only 23% are even considering trying something different by tak-ing risks, innovating, and changing how they lead inside their organizations.[1] When directly asked what is stopping these lead-ers from operating differently, the majority responded with con-cerns resulting from managing distributed teams, uncertainty regarding the right talent and skills mix given the unexpected entrance of generative AI, and general anxiety surrounding the macroeconomic conditions we face today. Simply stated, many don't know where to start.

Their predicament is as understandable as it is perilous. We know from our daily engagement with CEOs across the Global 500 that many business leaders are themselves overwhelmed and exhausted, unable to pivot fast enough to stay ahead of the chaotic and shifting disruptions of the pandemic, emerging technologies, supply chain issues, inflation, and growing political tensions at home and abroad. CEOs, like their employees, have discovered the limits of their resilience. Many simply have given up.

This is more than just a serious morale problem. It is an eco-nomic time bomb, accounting for $8.8 trillion in lost productiv-ity.[2] Yet CEOs tend to be more concerned with their company being continually productive than with setting policies and prac-tices to help workers avoid burnout and exhaustion, apparently unaware of the cause-and-effect between the two.

As these and other data reveal, seeing workers as human beings first and factors of production second isn't simply an enlightened approach to management. It is an economic imperative. Stakeholders are no longer willing or required to put up with the refusal of leaders to share power, collaborate openly, or embrace the values of those who do the heavy lifting.

Some confuse a human-powered approach with being more humane – being nicer – a dangerous oversimplification of the real crisis they face. Worse, many willfully reject the idea that they need to do anything at all, clutching at the false hope that somehow the seismic shifts of the last few decades will simply go away.

And while the costs of implementing a human-powered approach to management may appear significant, especially at the beginning, they are far outweighed by the potential benefits. The Upwork Research Institute ran a study in 2023 to determine the impact having a human-centric workplace made on a company's bottom line (see Figure I.1). The implications for leaders today are astounding.

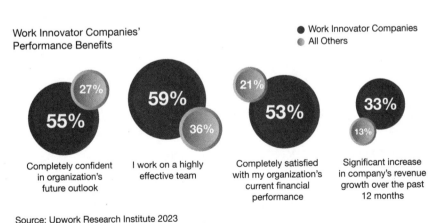

FIGURE I.1 Human-powered leadership practices pay off.

We wrote this book for the next generation of leaders and those now in power who recognize that something must change – and soon – if we are to make progress of any kind. Our intention is to understand and use history alongside the latest research to inform what's needed from organizations now to drive business forward into the future. Together with our shared experience working with leaders and executives across industries, countries, and enterprises of all sizes and ages, we're redefining what it means to be a leader in the twenty-first century, making the case that the only way forward, for the good of people and for business, is to radically transform the way we manage. Our hope is that you'll walk away from *Essential* with a new understanding of the needs, motivations, and potential of your own workforce, inspired to change what you can for them to thrive.

I

The Business Imperative for Human-Powered Leadership

1

The Economics of Human-Powered Leadership

"People follow leaders by choice. Without trust, at best you get compliance."

—Jesse Lyn Stoner[1]

As researchers we have a great appreciation for the lessons of our past and how they shape our present and future. We rely on historical perspectives to understand how organizations and the economy have evolved in response to advances in technology, automation, and machines over time, which have in turn informed employee capability and skills requirements. In this chapter, we examine how technological advances have shifted the power dynamics between employers and employees, widened the skills gap, and presented new socioeconomic challenges that require us to reexamine our leadership. So please bear with the history lessons because they are critical to the foundational argument of

the book – that humans must be at the center of our organizations for our societies and the global economy to flourish into
the future.

A Brief History of Organizational Evolution: How We Got Here

Where is here exactly? The pandemic, a growing consumer
demand for more sustainable products and business models, and
the rapid embrace of stakeholder capitalism more generally have
all accelerated three long-term macroeconomic trends: flattened
organizations, the democratization of data, and skills scarcity.
(Stakeholder capitalism assumes the purpose of business is for
more than maximizing shareholder profits and seeks to add value
to stakeholders such as society, employees, and vendors.) These
forces translate into specific organizational shifts that leaders are
now navigating, largely without a playbook. Taken together, they
create the business imperative to reexamine our organizations
and leaders with new criteria that put humans at the center of the
way we work, prioritize, and make decisions.

Decades of top-down management theory have been upended
in recent years in favor of the flattened organization – it's simply
too costly to design today's workplace around hierarchical structures. As a result, decision-making is very often conducted from
the bottom up, with workers driving innovation and collaboration and using it to take collective action. This trend is spurred
on by the fact that workers today often know more than their
leaders about how work actually gets done. Most leaders lack a
basic knowledge of the technology used to drive their business
forward, and as data and knowledge are increasingly democratized, those working closest to it hold the most power and influence. In today's digital environment, it is the insights gleaned,
not the data itself, that is most valuable.

With these factors at play, and no longer being limited to seek employment locally, highly skilled workers are empowered in ways never seen before to capitalize on career opportunities. But these circumstances, while favorable for some, create a growing concern for those workers unable to keep up with market demands. An imbalance in the supply and demand of talent has created a skills gap that is costing both businesses and society trillions of dollars. It is arguably the most urgent problem facing our organizations today.

The impact of these trends on the global economy illuminates a need for organizational change that shifts focus from asset management to talent management. Put another way, the power dynamic has changed polarities, giving leverage to stakeholders at the expense of enterprises.

In 2023 alone, we've seen how this shift has changed the game for leaders. Take, for example, the leverage UPS drivers had in negotiating higher rates and better working conditions. Due to the low unemployment rates and lack of available workers, leadership at UPS did not have much leverage in negotiating and gave the workforce most of what they demanded, including higher wage rates and better workplace conditions.[2] Or consider the example of Open AI, whose CEO was ousted, only to be reinstated days later when nearly the entire employee population threatened to quit. Finally, in the hotly debated return-to-office movement, we see that workers still have the upper hand as many refuse to adhere to their leaders' call for a return to office.

A human-first approach to business is not simply the popular or politically expedient thing to do. Neither is it merely a change in rhetoric for management to sound more empathetic and appeal to the zeitgeist. Genuine change is required – and hard to achieve – for the continued growth of our organizations and the health of the global economy.

Zeroing in on Profit and Productivity

Our brief history lesson starts with the First Industrial Revolution in the late eighteenth to early nineteenth centuries, during which organizations primarily focused on efficiency, productivity, and mass production. As you may well know, the introduction of factories and machinery led to the emergence of large-scale manufacturing, with organizations structured around hierarchical and centralized systems of control for the first time. This way of working required specific roles from people to manage the mass production of products in a brand-new way. During this period, we saw the rise of manufacturing companies, such as DuPont, Ford, and Boston Manufacturing.[3]

The leading economist and management thinker of the eighteenth century, Adam Smith, believed a division of labor was necessary to reduce the costs of goods that resulted from newfound global demand. As a result, there was a steep decline in training people for a "trade" or "craft" – instead, these newly formed organizations sought workers to fulfill a narrow and specific task within a large production line. The birth of management transpired as companies realized they needed a new role within their organization to coordinate the array of people now working on specialized and interdependent tasks along the production line.

The advantages of this new way of working were clear from a traditional economics perspective. Goods and services could now be made at scale, servicing new global customers as well as ensuring a level of standardization otherwise unachievable. The disadvantages to the human worker were also profound. Without a direct connection to the customer or product, it quickly became unclear what should motivate people tasked with the same repetitive workday. Workers during this time often lamented their boss's capricious management style, the result of inadequate training to understand and meet core human needs – ones we all share, regardless of which century we live in.[4]

A leading railroad analyst at this time, Henry Varnum Poor, cautioned of the dangers that this change in work was having on people. He warned, "Regarding man as a mere machine, out of which all the qualities necessary to be a good servant can be enforced by the mere payment of wages, may not work, as duties cannot always be prescribed, and the most valuable are often voluntary ones."[5]

How We Became "Cogs in a Wheel"

This First Industrial Revolution gave way to Frederick Taylor's and others' examination of scientific management in the late nineteenth and early twentieth century. The principles of this approach are characterized by a focus on engineering, optimizing, and standardizing work processes and tasks to achieve greater efficiency and productivity, from which we saw the rise of specialized job roles and detailed job descriptions.

During this period, the phrase "cog in a wheel" became a well-known way to describe how most workers felt under Taylor's relentless focus to break down jobs further into small discrete tasks that would be aggressively measured for productivity. (While the concept of the cog in a wheel originated in the fifteenth century, its use as applied to workers became mainstream in the 1930s.) What ensued is described by the twentieth-century management thinker Whiting Williams as "the worst time in history" for labor relations.[6] In 1919, more than four million American workers, or 20% of the nation's workforce, went on strike.[7] Turnover at leading companies, such as the Ford Motor Company, reached 380% with 10% daily absentee rates of their workforce.[8] The lack of human-centric management was costing the already fragile US economy. As a result, the government formed an Industrial Relations committee to better understand the state of labor and how this new scientific management was influencing talent.

Their conclusion? That the system operated with a complete disregard for employee welfare for the sake of profit, and in the process denied employees a say in the standards of their own working conditions. Under these circumstances, the report concluded, there would be no reason for workers to endorse or support a system that "[reduces] them to mere soulless machinery, mechanical in action, denuded of thought, and which would rob them of their humanhood."[9]

What Motivates Us?

Ultimately, the report deemed scientific management ill-equipped to move the economy forward, and with more attention paid to job roles and competencies, an examination of what having a workforce of employees really means began. The Human Relations Movement in the early to mid-twentieth century thus shifted the focus of organizations toward understanding the social and psychological aspects of work and its influence on optimizing work processes in the management of humans. It's during this period that we see organizations start to recognize the importance of employee satisfaction, motivation, and morale in improving productivity and performance.

The most famous thinker to emerge during this time was Elton Mayo, who like Frederick Taylor believed scientific experiments were needed in the workplace to better understand and improve human performance; with the field of management still in its infancy, managers needed training and data to effectively lead their workforces. However, unlike Taylor, Mayo placed an emphasis on deeply understanding what motivates humans rather than what drives profits. His work profoundly shifted management thinking at this time, with research that demonstrated productivity increases when individuals feel connected to others within their work group, are asked for their input through employee listening activities, and are given a purpose for their work. The summary of his research, produced in the late 1930s, stated the role of a manager was not to drive efficiencies, but to manage relationships.[10]

It's All About Perspective

Organizational development emerged as a field of study in the mid-twentieth century because of Mayo's work. It brought with it even more attention to improving organizational effectiveness and employee well-being through deep dives into culture, leadership, and employee engagement. It's at this point we see companies begin to emphasize teamwork, participative decision-making, and employee development.

Douglas McGregor was the leading contributor to the management field at this time. His research focused on the organizational culture that leaders must facilitate to drive greater human performance. In the 1960s, Dr. McGregor realized that managers led very differently depending on core assumptions they held about their workforce. He came up with Theory X to describe managers who exert a "command-and-control" style of leadership because of an underlying belief that people fundamentally don't want to work. Their role was to align divergent worker interests by means of compliance. In contrast, Theory Y managers supported and actively developed people because they believed that they inherently do want to work. A Theory Y manager's role was simply to nurture and support the development of people wanting to contribute back to the organization.

These two leadership beliefs are still at play today – you may have very well worked under a "command-and-control" leader at some point in your career. In fact, Upwork Research found that approximately one in four global leaders today said they do not trust their workforce to do what's right for the organization.[11]

It's Not You, It's the System

With newfound understanding of workforce motivations and management styles, total quality management (TQM) and continuous improvement methodologies gained prominence, emphasizing quality, customer satisfaction, and process improvement. During this movement, organizations focused on empowering employees to identify and solve problems proactively and fostering a culture of continuous learning and improvement.

Dr. W. Edwards Deming emerged as TQM's great thinker. He elevated the conversation on performance by expanding it from an assessment of individual factors to an evaluation of operating systems. His novel approach encouraged managers to look at an organization's entire ecosystem to identify connections and interactions that could cause friction for human performance. Deming then introduced the 94–6 rule, which attributes 94% of all challenges and needs for improvement to the system, under the responsibility of management, and only 6% to individual performance factors.[12] He famously stated, "A bad system will beat a good person every time."

Under this framework, managers would need to take a new approach to fully understand their organizational system and its influence on productivity. It requires them to listen to and empower frontline workers to solve problems in real time, rather than rely on top-down instructions from those farthest away from the work – as had been the norm in hierarchical chains of command. Deming argued that to be effective, improvements to the way we work must be pulled from those closest to the customer or problem at hand. His work within Toyota ushered in a new era of workforce empowerment, as the company emerged as a leader in high-quality car manufacturing because of its emphasis on workforce listening and enabling frontline workers to make process improvements in real time. Research shows that the company, on average, implements nine ideas per employee a year.[13]

Toyota's rise to prominence comes as no surprise. Leaders who implement workforce listening practices ultimately empower continuous employee innovation, no matter their role within the organization. Within this culture, workers are enabled to identify solutions to problems that often live outside the purview of leadership. As more organizations benefited from the practice of fueling innovation from the frontlines, a new era of management emerged that shifted focus from systems-based efficiencies to workforce empowerment, innovation, and new ways of working.

Teams at the Center

With success stories like Toyota, organizations recognized the potential for employees to advance their products and services and drive business value. At the same time, the rise of technology and globalization in the latter half of the twentieth century put a sharp focus on innovation and the emerging knowledge economy. The famous management consultant Peter Drucker first coined the idea of the knowledge economy back in 1969 when he realized that business value was increasingly moving toward the production of intangibles within organizations, with human cognition as the key driver of economic development.

But it wasn't until the mid-1990s that we saw the knowledge economy in full swing, with a company's intangible assets overtaking the balance sheet, compared to their tangible assets. To further spur innovation, companies started to champion agility, adaptability, and collaboration, with an emphasis on leveraging intellectual capital, encouraging creativity, and fostering a learning culture. It was at this point that Herbert Simon, a longtime authority on organizational design and a staunch believer in hierarchy, changed his long-held views to describe the role of managers as excelling at the delegation of decision-making to their workforce.[14]

As these models harnessed the collective intelligence of employees and put teams at the center of growth and progress, it became clear that management styles and capabilities also had to change. The heretofore command-and-control, hierarchical style of management was not a one-size-fits-all model. Leaders' behavior and style of management had to evolve in significant ways (see Figure 1.1)

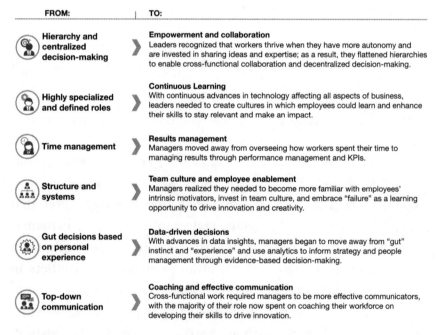

FROM:	TO:
Hierarchy and centralized decision-making	**Empowerment and collaboration** Leaders recognized that workers thrive when they have more autonomy and are invested in sharing ideas and expertise; as a result, they flattened hierarchies to enable cross-functional collaboration and decentralized decision-making.
Highly specialized and defined roles	**Continuous Learning** With continuous advances in technology affecting all aspects of business, leaders needed to create cultures in which employees could learn and enhance their skills to stay relevant and make an impact.
Time management	**Results management** Managers moved away from overseeing how workers spent their time to managing results through performance management and KPIs.
Structure and systems	**Team culture and employee enablement** Managers realized they needed to become more familiar with employees' intrinsic motivators, invest in team culture, and embrace "failure" as a learning opportunity to drive innovation and creativity.
Gut decisions based on personal experience	**Data-driven decisions** With advances in data insights, managers began to move away from "gut" instinct and "experience" and use analytics to inform strategy and people management through evidence-based decision-making.
Top-down communication	**Coaching and effective communication** Cross-functional work required managers to be more effective communicators, with the majority of their role now spent on coaching their workforce on developing their skills to drive innovation.

FIGURE 1.1 Key shifting in management capabilities.

These changes in the manager–employee relationship necessitated a more sophisticated management capability. Managers now needed to understand employees beyond just their technical acumen – they also needed to uncover their personal motivations at work and create conditions and a culture that enabled optimal productivity and boosted the engagement of their teams.

As a result of a move toward team-based performance optimization, the daily responsibilities of managers changed dramatically. Research conducted in 2016 found that "time spent by managers and their employees in collaborative activities has ballooned by 50 percent or more" over the past two decades.[15] Additional research suggests that 75% percent of a worker's time is spent communicating with others. The central question for leaders therefore became: How do I best enable the flow of communication and knowledge-sharing among my team members?

In 2012, Google led the charge to answer this question with data. Through their study called Project Aristotle, they sought to better understand why some teams stumbled while others soared in performance.[16] At first, they focused on structure and composition, trying to determine the makeup of a high-performing team. The problem was that their data showed no patterns when it came to team composition. Something else must be happening to explain why some managers were leading teams that work better than others.

After a year of study, the group of researchers discovered that group norms and team culture mattered most to performance. And the group norm that carried the most weight? Having team rules of operating in place that allowed individual members to feel psychologically safe. Author Dr. Amy Edmondson defines psychological safety as a "shared belief held by members of a team that the team is safe for interpersonal risk-taking. It describes a team climate characterized by interpersonal trust and mutual respect in which people are comfortable being themselves."[17]

With these new insights, a manager's role quickly evolved beyond just listening to and empowering individuals to solve problems in real time – it now included enabling the flow of information and effective collaboration between team members by creating an environment of psychological safety. The management of processes and mechanics was therefore of much less concern than the critical responsibility of managing relationships, skills, and teaming. Managers, no longer able to motivate people to work together through hierarchical power structures, had to facilitate the right culture within their organizations to enable the flow of skills, talent, and ideas without friction.

Where We Are Now: A Skills-Based Economy Emerges

We've seen companies evolve over the course of history from a sole focus on efficiency and productivity in the manufacturing of goods and services, to an emphasis on collaboration, knowledge, and creativity to fuel innovation. At the center of this evolution has been the role of the employee, and their skills to drive business value and differentiation. In step with these changes, the manager has also developed over time from task driver to coach and enabler.

As we enter a new era of rapidly advancing technology, leaders are faced with a new challenge: to keep pace with our digital-everything world, they must facilitate the continuous development of their workforce's skills. There is no denying that technology informs where and how work gets done; so too must we accept that the role of leadership must evolve with the world around it if it is to stay relevant.

Consider this. Most of the largest global companies by market cap, even in the early 2000s, were those producing traditional goods and services. Yet by 2018 all the largest global companies by market cap were digital-first organizations, offering technology goods or services. Microsoft, Apple, Facebook (now Meta), Amazon, and Alphabet redefined how we think about value creation, in turn necessitating a new way to think about talent and the continued evolution of management. Today, studies estimate that 90% of all business value is now generated through intangible assets.[18]

While the rise in technology companies we see today is somewhat unprecedented, what isn't is the impact it's having on the workforce. Since the onset of computers entering the world of work, economists have observed what's called skill- biased technical change, meaning that the production and introduction of new technologies favor skilled workers over unskilled workers in terms of higher wages and opportunities. This means that those with lower skills are at a disadvantage when a new technology enters the workforce, often causing their job tasks to be automated or disrupted. (Note that skilled labor is defined by the level of specialized training required to complete the job. Unskilled labor, while still valuable, often does not require the same level of training.) The reason is that technology is often used to increase productivity of skilled workers and plays a role of augmentation, rather than substitution, for highly skilled talent. In addition, the creation and implementation of new technologies, such as cloud-computing, blockchain, and AI, require highly skilled workers. But as we will further explore, the speed of a skills-biased technology change is utterly dependent on the number of highly skilled workers entering the workforce. With the introduction of technologies like generative AI, we are yet again entering into new territory that will disrupt labor faster than people can keep up.

As a result of these advances, we're seeing a move toward the commoditization of jobs and skills. Commoditization occurs when a human skill becomes less unique because there is little differentiation between a person doing a task and technology doing the same one. Thomas Davenport asserts, "Jobs are increasingly viewed as undifferentiated and interchangeable across humans and machines – the very definition of a commodity. ... The value of many jobs is driven less by their intrinsic worth than by market demand."[19] We are seeing this in jobs that were once prized as human-only tasks, like writing or content creation, and are now being increasingly commodified by the onset of generative AI. For example, images created by an AI tool are often indistinguishable from what a human could create.

While technology has always disrupted the workforce, the implications of advances like generative AI and machine learning today present a unique leadership challenge: Skills are being commoditized at faster rates than people are entering the workplace with the necessary skills to work with new technology, creating what's known as skills scarcity. And yet, as an IBM executive recently remarked, skills are "the currency of the future."[20]

In this fast-paced environment where skills are as scarce a resource as any, we are no longer in an era defined by a "war for talent"; rather, we've entered a "war for skills" within the greater skills economy.

2

Skills Scarcity in the Digital Age

"A.I. could usher in a world of work that is anchored more, not less, around human ability."
 —Aneesh Raman and Maria Flynn, *New York Times*[1]

The shift toward a skills-based economy is profound for leadership. At the center of this development is the need for leaders to look differently at talent, how it is identified, and how it is engaged and leveraged within their organizations. To do so, they must understand the intersection of circumstances, trends, and dynamics at play that are contributing to the emerging skills scarcity dilemma. Within a rapidly changing market, economy, and culture, part of a leader's primary responsibility is to outfit their organization and equip their people with the right capabilities to stay competitive and drive innovation forward. In other words, if we are to avoid a true skills scarcity crisis, leaders must learn to put people first.

Understanding the Skills Scarcity Equation

The term "skills scarcity" has been used for quite some time, but only became popular during the early 2000s, when we began to see an increased demand for highly skilled workers across what are traditionally referred to as white-collar and blue-collar workers. White-collar roles have been those typically associated with office or knowledge work, while blue-collar roles are those associated with the trades or physical work. Research conducted by the ManPower Group, which looked at over 40,000 global employers, has identified an alarming and rising trend. In 2014, only 36% of global employers reported having trouble finding talent. Just 10 years later, in 2024, that percentage increased to 75%, or 3 out of every 4 global employers struggling to find the talent they need.[2] This challenge is most pronounced for organizations searching for talent with skills in IT and data, engineering, and manufacturing across nearly every industry and geography. And it's not just on the employer's side; in new research, a study found that 65% of workers today report they are not leveraging their greatest skill at work.[3]

Because of this skills shortage, management consulting company Korn Ferry estimates that technological disruption will equate to a talent shortage of 85 million people and cost the global economy an approximate $8.5 trillion by 2030.[4] The skills shortage is more than just an idea – it's a phenomenon that's costing our businesses and the growth of the broader economy.

To address and solve for its trillion-dollar corporate cost, it's important to understand what's driving skills scarcity and the demand for leaders to manage people in new ways. We see the intersection of four distinct factors, which we unpack through the rest of this chapter, driving the skills shortage we are facing today. Today's leader needs to recognize and manage the forces that are accelerating the skills scarcity within their organization, such as the decrease in the half-life of skills and overall declining workforce participation, as well as bolster efforts around skilling and new hiring practices to mitigate their effects. How these forces add up and relate to each other is best demonstrated through an equation, with forces driving as well as mitigating the skills scarcity crisis. As will be discovered, leaders' attention and energies should focus on the factors that mitigate skills scarcity to offset the broader macroeconomic forces at play in the labor markets (see Figure 2.1).

Each of these factors is changing the economics of talent management today. To address those changes, leaders must pay closer attention to the hidden, human forces beyond their balance sheets that are influencing their ability to remain competitive and agile. When we better understand what's driving skills scarcity, what's been historically considered sunk cost – for example, workforce training and development or efforts to increase diversity in hiring – ultimately become positive factors that help to offset broader economic developments outside of a leader's control.

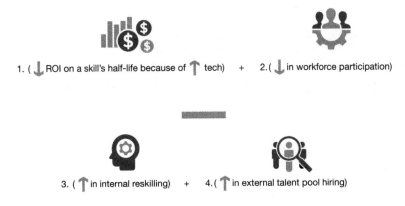

1. (⬇ ROI on a skill's half-life because of ⬆ tech) + 2. (⬇ in workforce participation)

3. (⬆ in internal reskilling) + 4. (⬆ in external talent pool hiring)

FIGURE 2.1 The skills scarcity equation.

Let's take a closer look at each of the four factors driving skills scarcity and explore real-life examples of how they influence the economics of talent today.

Technological Advances Decrease the Half-Life of Skills

A 2020 McKinsey study suggests that companies lack the talent they'll need to drive business forward in the future largely due to the disruption of technology: 44% of respondents said their organizations will face skill gaps within the next five years, and another 43% reported existing skill gaps (see Figure 2.2). In other words, 87% said they are either experiencing skills gaps now or expect them within a few years, and 3 in 10 shared that at least a quarter of their organization's roles are at risk of disruption in the next five years.[5]

The need for highly skilled workers across industries and verticals is only going to become more complex as the half-life of skills continues to decline. The World Economic Forum (WEF)

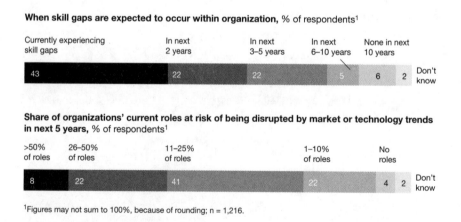

When skill gaps are expected to occur within organization, % of respondents[1]

Currently experiencing skill gaps	In next 2 years	In next 3–5 years	In next 6–10 years	None in next 10 years	
43	22	22	5	6	2 Don't know

Share of organizations' current roles at risk of being disrupted by market or technology trends in next 5 years, % of respondents[1]

>50% of roles	26–50% of roles	11–25% of roles	1–10% of roles	No roles	
8	22	41	22	4	2 Don't know

[1]Figures may not sum to 100%, because of rounding; n = 1,216.

Source: McKinsey & Company.

FIGURE 2.2 Overview of when skills gap is expected to occur in organizations and % of roles at risk.

forecasts that 44% of today's core skills will be disrupted in the next five years.[6] The fastest-growing skills are those that are related to analytical thinking, creativity, technology, and literacy, as well as AI and big data. The research from WEF finds the demand for these rising skills across nearly every industry.

Consider the unexpected rise of Open AI's ChatGPT-3 that was released in November 2022 as evidence of how skills continue to be disrupted as technology advances. While writing was a core skill that many experts believed could be automated at some point in the future, few forecasted the impact that the introduction of ChatGPT would have. A *Forbes* article published in July 2021 noted that while AI was rapidly developing, the technology was viewed as only semi-coherent, unable to piece together divergent pieces of information and unable to produce audio or video. The author concludes that because of these things, "AI is not going to replace writers anytime soon."[7]

It took only 10 months for that sentiment to become outdated and for the future of writers to become a here-and-now talent issue. Hollywood screenwriters went on a 148-day strike in direct response to the use of generative AI and its ability to write entire screenplays and generate video of such quality that it may be difficult to determine whether a human or AI created the work. This nearly overnight displacement of critical creative human skills caused 11,500 screenwriters to walk out until further guardrails were in place for AI's use in their industry. Many referred to this as a true existential crisis for an industry that was previously deemed somewhat safe due to its reliance on human creativity.

As technology continues to advance even faster than anticipated, a shortage in the necessary skills and qualifications to keep pace is not only a challenge for organizations but spans socioeconomic realities within the larger global market. The skills gap impacts tens of millions of people around the world, including both white-collar and blue-collar roles.

What's known as the "blue-collar economy" includes manufacturing, healthcare, construction, transportation, agriculture, and health services. These industries are the foundation from which our communities and businesses operate and, one could argue, provide a competitive advantage for companies and countries engaged in international trade and the global market. While a shortage of available skills in industries like healthcare and the trades may seem obvious and continues to be the focus of many organizations today, it would be irresponsible to simply walk past them. They rely heavily on a different type of skill set and continue to struggle in attracting and/or retaining employees.

In our digital age, there is rising concern that blue-collar workers and job categories will be displaced by automation, robots, and machine learning. Research suggests that today there are 126 robots per employee in manufacturing, surging from 66 robots per 10,000 employees in 2015. Not only that, but with the introduction of more robots into factories, we have seen wages decline by 0.42%.[8] Yet there is a way for leaders to offset this displacement: through human-centric technology investments.

Land O'Lakes is an example of a company transforming an industry by investing in technology for its farmers. This over-100-year-old organization seeks to innovate one of the oldest industries, farming and agriculture, through technology development. Weather accounts for 70% of what happens on a farm, and inconsistency in weather patterns, humans' relatively poor ability to predict them, and local variability has always proved challenging for the industry. This is an area where AI can help to augment, rather than automate, farmers' skills. Teddy Bekele, chief technology officer at Land O'Lakes, describes it this way: "If you are at break-even today, the technology gets you to a spot where farming is exciting – you become a profitable farm.

And you would not have to add more acres or put yourself at greater risk to get there. It just means you are making better-optimized decisions with the technology."[9] This example illustrates that while technology will in fact disrupt certain blue-collar jobs, it also presents new opportunities for role adaptation. The onus is on companies to invest in the reskilling of blue-collar workers to work with and alongside the machines that will inevitably be used to generate more productivity and efficiency.

Advances in technology have transformed industries, and therefore, which skills and capabilities are and will be in demand. The displacement of certain jobs and capabilities will result in a widening gap between job seekers and the new skills employers need. As the demand for new skills outpaces the supply of individuals with them, the skills gap will continue to grow.

Declining Workforce Participation Widens the Skills Gap

The skills gap is further complicated by a shift in demographics and the available talent pool in the market. An aging workforce, gender, the introduction of Gen Z, and a new set of expectations from this youngest set of employees have all played a role in the shortage. Let us look at each to better understand their influence.

The Aging Workforce

The global population is aging, and with it our workforce. At the end of this decade, 35 countries will have one out of every five individuals over the age of 65 (Baby Boomers), and by 2034 people aged 65 and older will outnumber those under 18 in major economies such as the United States, Europe, and Asia.[10] This development creates significant issues for organizations who have seen an exodus of Boomers from the workplace in recent years because they have either sought early retirement or had their roles made redundant. The loss of our workforce's largest demographic group comes at a significant cost to the economy and burden to the workforce. The University of Southern California projects the Medicare-eligible population in the US to have doubled in size by 2030, compared to 2000, with over 69 million retirees, costing $259.8 billion in annual care costs.[11] It is a truly unprecedented demographic shift.

For a long time, the number of workers per retiree was much higher, causing little concern for where the next wave of talent would come from as older generations aged out.[12] However, since the early 2000s the number of workers per retiree is dramatically shrinking, creating much concern about not only who will fill the roles, but also on how to transfer the skills and knowledge of one generation of workers to another.

We see this dynamic most pronounced in industries where Baby Boomers dominate, and the next generation is failing to enter at the same pace. (Note the other economic cost this is having on society because this trend places a great financial burden on the new generation of workers, who must carry the costs of a growing aging population.) Consider the construction industry, which is facing a trifecta of an aging population, slower entry of new workers, and rising demand, leading to profound skills and labor shortages. The Bureau of Labor Statistics (BLS) has forecasted construction to be one of the fastest-growing occupations between 2016 and 2026, gaining over 747,000 jobs in the US. Still, at the same time as Baby Boomers retire, the construction industry forecasts that only one person will enter as five retire out. This imbalance of talent is likely to translate into five million open construction positions soon.[13] In a very real sense, the labor shortage in this industry may translate to buildings, roads, and other structures failing to meet customer demand, making it critical for leaders to solve this source of skills scarcity today.

When we turn to traditional white-collar industries, such as technology and professional services, we see a different skills shortage for older populations. The continued rise of AI in business requires the workforce to quickly learn and master a new digital tool and ultimately a new way of working. We've navigated this countless times before in our modern workplace with the rise of the internet, cell phones, platforms, and even cloud computing. However, with this next wave of technological advances, most notably AI, we see an alarming digital divide across generations.

A divide is typical with the entry of a new technology, but this one is marked by distrust and concern from older generations that this new tool will not add value. Yet younger generations have eagerly embraced it, with a study showing that 70% of global Gen Zers regularly use generative AI today, while 68% of global Baby Boomers report never using the tool at all.[14] Overcoming an aging population's resistance to the next wave of technology transformation will be critical for leaders seeking to capture the full potential of AI in their workplaces.

Women

Women have served as a backbone to the growing US economy ever since World War II. A study conducted by McKinsey found that since the 1970s, the additional productive power of a growing women's workforce accounts for a quarter of today's GDP.[15] We know from decades of economic studies that women represent a very important lever for societal health and growth,[16] and yet the women's labor force participation rate peaked in 1999 around 60% and has since declined.[17]

In fact, women are participating in the labor force at the lowest rates since entering it in meaningful numbers in the 1970s. In the spring of 2020, 3.5 million mothers left their jobs, driving the labor force participation rate for working moms from around 70% to 55%.[18] While 76% of all American women aged 25–54 are in the workforce, this is far less than other developed economies. Sweden, for example, has 87% of this cohort participating within their workforce. If the US were to increase workforce participation rate closer to the average of 84%, the size of the entire US economy would grow by 3–4%.[19]

There are a few factors at play here that are contributing to women exiting the workforce. The first is that the global pandemic dramatically disrupted jobs in retail, education, and health services as well as hospitality. Women tend to outnumber men in these professions and were more likely to be impacted by layoffs during this time. Not just that, but women were more likely to experience extreme burnout and leave their jobs because of it. The US Chamber of Commerce found that one in three women were considering leaving their careers due to burnout in their profession.[20] Finally, the lack of access to healthcare has caused women to exit the workforce to take over the role of childcare. A primary reason women tend to opt out for childcare duties is that a woman's wages are about $172 less per week compared to men. While much progress has been made to accelerate women in the workforce, some have argued we have taken a step back since the pandemic and are at risk of losing the gains made.

Solving this source of skills scarcity requires leaders to engage in job and organizational culture redesign to attract a cohort that is leaving our workforce at alarming rates. This is especially important as women are now gaining higher-level degrees at higher rates than men, yet do not obtain high-level roles at the same rate as men do.[21] As the skills landscape continues to shift, leaders must work proactively to bring more women into the workforce.

Gen Z

A new generation of workers, Gen Z, is set to overtake the number of Baby Boomers in the workforce by the end of 2024, according to research by Glassdoor.[22] We'll feel this demographic shift across many organizations, as new workforce values and expectations are introduced along with the next generation of workers. This generation, too, faces a concerning skills gap as the world of work around them rapidly evolves. Research conducted by the Workforce Institute finds that 51% of Gen Zers do not believe that their educational system has helped prepare them for work.[23] This same study finds the following skills gap self-identified by Gen Z workers: 26% do not feel prepared for negotiating at work, 24% do not feel prepared to network with others, and 24% do not feel confident speaking in front of a crowd at work.

Much emphasis is put on the growth and need for digital skills for the future of work – an area where Gen Z will certainly add value. But along with digital know-how, there is just as much need in the workplace for what have often been called "soft skills": leveraging uniquely human capabilities to conduct business, such as interpersonal communication, influence, and creative thinking. In fact, the World Economic Forum believes that curiosity, lifelong learning, flexibility, self-awareness, and customer service will be the top 10 in-demand skills over the next five years.[24] With the rise of remote and distributed work, Gen Z continues to be at a disadvantage in seeking to acquire these evergreen human-to-human skills, so often learned through observation and time with their leaders.

Take, for example, a tech company that one of us consulted for that was struggling with onboarding and retaining Gen Zers. What was once a prized industry for younger workers was now, with the start of the pandemic, struggling to adjust their new hire practices in distributed work environments.

We discovered that the transfer of soft skills was what was proving difficult for these Gen Z workers in a remote-first culture. While they excelled in the technical aspect of work, the reality is that much of a software engineer's job today revolves around communication, teamwork, and stakeholder influence. This lack of soft skills transfer was costing the organization nearly five extra months for a new hire to reach full productivity within this generational cohort, meaning that what would normally take three months with previous hires was now taking nearly eight months.

A new generation of workers entering the market, combined with the increase of remote work adoption, means that companies must urgently address the growing soft skills gap. Moreover, Gen Z is actively looking to their manager to help close it for them, according to a study from the Workforce Institute that found 37% of Gen Zers would not tolerate an unsupportive manager who did not facilitate their development.[25]

Demographic shifts such as an aging workforce, declining participation of women in the workplace, and fewer people entering certain industries overall are contributing to the skills scarcity challenge we face today. In economic forecasting, the types of demographic challenges we just discussed are referred to as "givens." It is imperative that leaders acknowledge them and recognize their pivotal role in shaping the future economy and solving for the skills scarcity at hand.

Reskilling to Balance Talent Supply and Demand

As advances in technology decrease the half-life of skills and demographic shifts further fuel the skills gap, upskilling and reskilling the workforce en masse becomes crucial.

The World Economic Forum believes that 50% of the workforce will have to reskill by 2025.[26] Today, inadequate training and education programs fail to equip individuals with the necessary skills for specific roles. This could include a lack of access to quality educational resources or a mismatch between the skills taught and those in demand by employers. These realities pose long-term issues for employers who are already struggling to keep up with the technological advances changing their competitive positioning in the market.

Every company is or will evolve to be a technology-defined or -dependent business, and the rapid and ever-evolving advancements in tech create a constant need for new skills. In the process, both companies and individuals alike will find themselves with outdated or insufficient skills to meet customer or other stakeholder demands. New industry capabilities – such as data science, AI, cybersecurity, digital marketing, and more – are now required within every organization across every aspect of the business. This development fundamentally changes the skills makeup of the talent, structure, and operating models needed for competitive advantage. But there is a silver lining. Advances in technology and the digital age have led to a democratization of information and knowledge. With the rise of online learning platforms and greater access to information in general, employers can develop, reskill, and upskill their employee base.

Take Schneider Electric as an example of longevity. Founded in 1836, it currently leads the industry in energy management and automation. In an era when business survival rates are under 20 years, Schneider Electric's long-term success is admirable.[27] This in part may be explained by their attention and focus on skilling within their organization, keeping them ahead of the skills gap.

But recently, an internal retention study found that 50% of all employees leaving Schneider Electric voluntarily were primarily driven by a lack of internal growth opportunities. The leadership team knew this was something they could address, but they'd first need to identify the skills gaps within their own organization. And so they turned to AI to leverage an internal marketplace platform (a digital tool that allows organizations to match their workers' skills and interests with relevant projects, tasks, or job opportunities at their company) that would give them better visibility into the existing skills within their organization and where those skills could be used in order to match worker capabilities with business needs. Jean Pelletier, the VP of digital transformation, reflected, "What I am learning is that it's a complete rewrite of HR. You need to think differently about speed and how you go deep and broad in an organization using AI."[28] The proof was in the results. These efforts to intentionally upskill their workforce with better skill matching resulted in $15 million and 360,000 working hours saved from reduced external recruiting costs.

Solving the skills scarcity crisis will take rewriting most of what you know about your own workforce and making visible the often hidden currency within your organization – human skills. The playbook many leaders were handed starting from the Industrial Revolution assumes that businesses gain efficiencies by training toward repeatable and scalable tasks. Tomorrow's leaders must follow a new playbook, grounded in the assumption that continued growth and success relies on ongoing skill renewal within their workforce. The companies that commit to this method, by investing in people and new tools like AI skills-matching platforms, are sure to gain an advantage in the new economy of talent.

Redefining and Expanding the Talent Pool

If we are being honest, part of the skills scarcity facing organizations is self-inflicted because of how we think about "top talent." Often, leaders limit an already scarce talent pool through qualification requirements and outdated assumptions about where top talent comes from, restricting the labor markets even further. What emerges is the rise of the "unicorn job," a role that is so packed with requirements that it's nearly impossible for a single individual to be qualified. This predicament requires us to redefine how we think about adding skills for our workforce and expand the talent pool itself.

The Rise of the Unicorn Job

In today's rapidly evolving job market, the rise of the "unicorn job" is reshaping the expectations of what leaders demand from their workforce. This hybrid role uniquely demands both technological competencies and creative thinking, creating a blend that was unimaginable just a few years ago. Research from Gartner underscores this transformation, revealing a dramatic 10% annual increase in the number of skills listed per job. Moreover, skills deemed essential a mere three years ago are now obsolete, emphasizing the relentless pace of change and the necessity for continuous upskilling. Workers are acutely feeling this shift, particularly in areas such as coding and traditional marketing, as AI and machine learning drive the demand for more advanced technical skills alongside strategic thinking capabilities.

This shift is further highlighted by the World Economic Forum's 2023 Future of Jobs Report, which predicts that nearly half of all core skills will be disrupted by 2027. The convergence of technology and human-centric skills, such as analytical and creative thinking, positions the unicorn job at the forefront of this new era. Companies are increasingly seeking individuals who not only understand complex technologies like AI and big data but can also apply creative solutions to novel problems. This dual demand is not just a trend but a fundamental shift in what leaders expect from their workforce.

As a result, companies are challenged by finding a candidate from the small pool of skilled individuals available for these unicorn jobs. This scarcity can be particularly prevalent in emerging fields or industries that require specialized expertise. Research conducted by the Harvard Business School found that more than 90% of employers who use recruiting management systems apply initial filters that screen out candidates who do not have "middle-skills" and "high-skills."[29] These are the types of skills that require access to specialized training after high school and can be costly to obtain, further perpetuating the perception of a lack of available talent. In reality we have to ask ourselves: Are we expecting too much from unicorn jobs? To bridge this gap, companies and educational institutions must collaborate to create more affordable and accessible training programs, ensuring a broader talent pool that can meet these evolving demands.

Resistance to External Talent Pools

In addition to impossible hiring standards for new roles, skills scarcity is driven by leaders who overlook the alternative workforce as a viable talent pool. In a somewhat surprising finding by the Upwork Research Institute, only 69% of leaders said they were willing to work with the highest-quality talent if it meant bringing them in as a freelancer or contractor.[30] The bias toward full-time employment options further limits leaders in identifying the right talent (i.e., skills) for their needs.

In fact, in the US, freelancing has been on the rise, with over 38% of the US workforce engaging in some form of freelance work. Furthermore, 94% of US growth from 2005 to 2015 was entirely made up of alternative workforce arrangements. And while many leaders may not think of freelancers as highly skilled workers, the reality is that the highest-paying and highest-skilled work is growing fastest among the alternative workforce.[31]

The economic impact of this trend is profound. Research shows that American freelancers contributed approximately $1.27 trillion in annual earnings to the US economy in 2023.[32]

While companies are making efforts to expand their reach to find talent (e.g. via high school, associate programs, and philanthropy), these efforts are simply not enough to meet the growing needs for skilled labor. Closing the skills gap starts with leaders changing their mindset and transforming how their organizations think about and approach talent acquisition. As will be discovered, human intelligence does not discriminate and can be found across talent pools that often get overlooked today.

Changing the Way We Think About Workforce Skills

The big question is: How do leaders reframe skills to stay ahead? A key challenge to navigating this question is how we have historically categorized, and therefore limited, our workforce in a way that no longer serves us. By defining jobs as either white- or blue-collar, our current framework operates under an overly simplified and bifurcated understanding of skills themselves. The fact is, technology is actively disrupting how we think about jobs in both categories, creating skills scarcity for all workers, and redefining how we work from the frontlines through the C-suite.

The auto industry is a good example of how our understanding of white- versus blue-collar work is changing. The industry has historically created traditional blue-collar work and relied heavily on manufacturing skills. But as Chad Mountray, chief economist at the National Association of Manufacturers points out, "There's no such thing as a low-skilled job in manufacturing anymore. To really thrive, we are going to need continuous learning and upskilling."[33]

The transition from making engines to electric vehicles powered by AI and sensors has completely upended the skills needed in manufacturing. Jacqueline Floro-Forde, VP of human resources at Panasonic, stated, "Challenges associated with transforming the automotive industry from internal combustion engines to electric have driven skills shortages. We always need engineers, but we also need people who understand data and how it feeds improvements."[34]

The evolution in the types of skills needed today for traditional blue-collar industries is profound. It's therefore necessary to introduce a new category of work to understand the convergence of these categories of skills, which until now were largely separate. Tom O'Reilly, VP at Rockwell Automation, describes it this way: "To maximize sustainability and productivity, you need skills that marry the physical and digital worlds: namely, you need the ability to deal with cloud-based software and the ability to understand applications and interactions between mechanical and automation systems."

The implications of this growing expectation for our current blue-collar workforce are alarming. Research shows that while the highest-skilled workers continue to develop through skills-biased technology change, the number of jobs for middle-skilled workers gradually decreases.[35] Their roles are being replaced by more highly skilled workers as robotization increases across many blue-collar professions. Those who can work between the physical and digital worlds will flourish, but these types of skilled workers are few and far between.

Furthermore, certain white-collar professionals who have typically been considered "safe" from being made redundant by technological advancement are now at most risk. The World Economic Forum suggests that 40% of knowledge workers' hours will be disrupted by generative AI in the coming years.[36] This displacement is of course predicted to be offset by highly skilled work in the emerging fields of data science, analytics, and machine learning science, but is still important to consider.

The changes to skill requirements across the entire workforce require us to define this need for a third category of workers more clearly (see Figure 2.3). They are neither white-collar nor blue-collar and, due to sociopolitical and economic circumstances, have remained either invisible to the market or lacked the access and infrastructure to enter our evaluation process. As a result, we have not yet determined skill sets or developed apprentice and education programs around them. But if businesses and our larger economy are to thrive, there is an urgent need to recognize and support this important category emerging in our workforce: the "gray-collar" worker. They span all sectors from manufacturing and retail to administrative roles, transportation, media, and more. Many workers will be displaced, but the question remains whether companies and communities can and will build their capabilities and invest in upskilling or reskilling these valuable individuals in our workforce.

Gray-collar workers occupy a unique position in the labor market, straddling the traditional boundaries between blue-collar (manual labor) and white-collar (office work) roles. These jobs often involve a combination of technical skill, specialized knowledge, and physical work, and are found in industries such

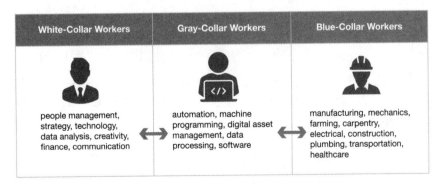

FIGURE 2.3 Comparison of white-, gray-, and blue-collar workers.

as healthcare, technology, and skilled trades. Examples include technicians, paramedics, and craftspeople. As artificial intelligence (AI) and automation technologies advance, the future of gray-collar employment and its susceptibility to automation is a topic of growing interest and concern.

Addressing the challenges of the skills economy requires a proactive approach, including continuous learning and upskilling, targeted training programs, and collaboration between educational institutions, healthcare workers, employers, and policymakers to ensure that our workforce is equipped with the necessary capabilities for the digital era. But beyond solving for skills scarcity to meet the demands of our economy, the future of business relies on the continued evolution of our management practices to center people within our organizations, and within our technology. Companies must reevaluate not only how they acquire and build skilled workforces, but how they fundamentally invest in, relate to, and engage their employees for them to flourish and add value far into the future.

A Call to Action for Future Leaders

The profound economic implications of our current leadership conundrum boil down to a pressing need to address the skills gap that is wreaking havoc across sectors. We find ourselves grappling with formidable external forces: a dwindling pool of talent and the rapidly diminishing lifespan of skills. Yet it is within a leader's grasp to counteract these challenges by broadening the horizons of talent acquisition and committing to the continuous development of their teams.

The stakes transcend mere financial losses, which are already projected to soar into the trillions; they touch upon the very fabric of our work–life stability. The societal toll of job disruption – marked by pervasive uncertainty and loss of income – is immense. To mitigate this, it is imperative for leaders to transcend the outdated dichotomy of technology versus humanity and inaugurate a new way to think about management and leadership that centers around leveraging human intelligence alongside advances in artificial intelligence. This is what will define the next era of leadership theory and practice (see Figure 2.4).

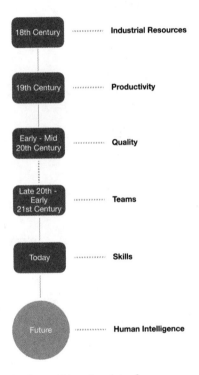

FIGURE 2.4 The evolution of leadership focus.

Addressing these challenges is not only a responsibility but a defining characteristic of contemporary leadership, propelling both individuals and enterprises toward a revolutionary future of work. The critical inquiry now is this: How can leaders overhaul decades of entrenched business practices to pave the way for a leadership paradigm that truly reflects the essence of business? This paradigm must not only generate economic value for the elite but also enrich society. The call to action is urgent; it demands that leaders not only envision but actively forge a path toward work that is more meaningful, inclusive, and fundamentally human-powered.

3

Investing in Human Intelligence

"The true sign of intelligence is not knowledge but imagination."
—Albert Einstein[1]

We find ourselves at a critical juncture in the economic evolution at which we must define the relationship between humans and technology. Nearly every industry and every type of work will be actively disrupted by technological advances if they have not been already. We've seen, for example, the impact robotics has made on augmenting physical labor in our workforce, and how artificial intelligence has enhanced knowledge work. As new technologies continue to be adopted into our workplaces, we are forced to confront questions about how to move workers up the value chain alongside innovation, and moreover to solve for how we will center humanity in the further development of artificial intelligence.

While some see the arrival of so-called "generative AI" as the biggest threat to workers since the introduction of robots into factories, we have a different outlook. (Generative AI is a type of artificial intelligence capable of creating high-quality content, such as text, images, and video, based on patterns and structures learned from existing data.) AI indeed transforms the nature of work, but human intelligence (i.e., the cognitive strengths that are unique to our species) remains irreplaceable. Work itself must be redesigned to bring together the complementary capabilities of human and machine in a way that benefits business and people. In fact, it's our view that over time AI and other automation technologies have the potential to make work more human – not less – by freeing up time and energy for workers to focus on uniquely human capabilities such as creativity and judgment. That is, if leaders value, nurture, and prioritize these skills.

For far too long, leaders have focused on developing technology and AI at the expense of human intelligence – and even humanity itself. As a result, we are often presented with the false dichotomy that the future of work is either human or machine but cannot be both. However, the next era of leadership will in fact center around unlocking, creating, and leveraging human intelligence in the workplace in relationship with technology, rather than in competition. To do so effectively, it's imperative for leaders to gain a better understanding of the strengths (and limitations) of each.

Artificial Intelligence: Made in Our Likeness

There's no doubt that much of the fear regarding the technological disruption of our workforce is real. Headlines abound about how AI is coming for most workers today, with many experts projecting profound job loss. It is not that we do not believe that

AI will disrupt the way we work, but we do believe that many of these fears are overstated and take the view that there's nothing we can do to mitigate it. The fact is, just like tech innovations that came before, in many cases the strengths of AI are limited without the application of human intelligence alongside them.

To understand this better, let us demystify what artificial intelligence is and begin to unpack where its strengths begin and end. In effect, AI serves as a simulation of various aspects of human intelligence processes but carried out by machines, especially computer systems, with the goal of enabling them to perform tasks such as visual perception, speech recognition, decision-making, and language translation. Its processes include learning (the acquisition of information and rules for using the information), reasoning (using rules to reach approximate or definite conclusions), and self-correction. The backbone of AI is machine learning, a subset of the technology that focuses on developing computer programs that can access data and use it to learn for themselves. Foundational to machine learning is the idea that systems can learn from data, identify patterns, and make decisions with minimal human intervention. Many leaders often confuse generative AI advancements (such as ChatGPT), which create new content based on vast amounts of broad datasets, with machine learning (such as facial recognition), which considers data patterns and provides predictive analysis within a particular context or domain.

AI excels when large datasets of past behaviors are available and can appear intelligent within this confined context. When these parameters are met, AI's capabilities boast significant advantages in data processing, pattern recognition, and automation. The unparalleled ability to process and analyze vast amounts of data reaches far beyond human capability and enables organizations to derive meaningful insights for better decision-making, innovation, and competitive advantage. Likewise, pattern recognition through machine learning helps to reveal patterns and anomalies with remarkable accuracy, crucial in various applications from fraud detection in the financial industry to diagnostic imaging in healthcare. By recognizing these patterns, AI can also predict outcomes, allowing organizations to anticipate and respond proactively to future scenarios. And lastly, the automation of performing repetitive tasks more quickly, accurately, and tirelessly than human workers is transforming industries. This automation ranges from simple tasks, such as data entry, to more complex processes, such as manufacturing and quality control. By automating these routine tasks, AI allows humans to focus on higher-level, creative, and strategic activities, leading to increased productivity and innovation. These three strengths are critical for leaders to understand if they are to implement the technology in ways that are effective for businesses and their people.

Ultimately, artificial intelligence represents a pinnacle of technological advancement. It has already made a significant impact across various sectors, and as we look to the future the synergy between human and artificial intelligence holds the promise of unprecedented opportunities to enhance our capabilities and pave the way for innovations we can scarcely imagine today. By embracing AI, we stand on the cusp of a new era of progress, one where technology not only amplifies our own human abilities but also inspires us to reach new heights of achievement and understand ourselves. But to realize these benefits, leaders must first identify, value, and build human intelligence with the same interest, passion, and urgency.

Why Technology Needs Humans

While AI is promised to usher in a new era of productivity based on its capabilities, leaders are confronted with what is known as the "productivity paradox." This term encapsulates the curious observation that despite the exponential growth in technology and innovation, productivity growth – particularly in developed economies – has not kept pace. This paradox is a critical puzzle for business leaders to solve, one that demands a nuanced understanding and strategic response.

At its core, the productivity paradox challenges the conventional wisdom that advancements in technology directly translate to increased productivity and, by extension, economic growth. Since the late twentieth century, despite the digital revolution transforming how businesses operate, the expected surge in productivity has been elusive. This discrepancy raises important questions about the nature of technological progress and its real-world impacts. First and foremost, it underscores the complexity of technology adoption and challenges the idea that simply investing in the latest tools and platforms is a panacea for productivity challenges. Instead, it proves that it must be effectively integrated into workflows, and employees need to be adept at leveraging these tools to enhance their work. The human element – how individuals interact with technology – plays a pivotal role in unlocking productivity gains.

To combat this paradox, leaders must realize where humans excel over machines, and that these advantages amount to more than just the token human traits of creativity and empathy. While these are indeed uniquely human characteristics, there is a more nuanced and profound difference that enables us to recognize where human intelligence lives in an AI-driven world. In the realm of technology and human capability, the core insight that has emerged with resounding clarity is that human intelligence is fundamentally characterized by its depth in emotion, context, and judgment. This contrasts starkly with AI, which, despite its advancements, remains inherently linear, sterile, and heavily reliant on vast repositories of historical data, so far incapable of replicating these subtle dimensions of human cognition. When it comes to forming predictions and making decisions, the distinction between the two forms of intelligence is quite remarkable, and leaders seeking to unlock both in their organizations would be wise to consider how to leverage each strength appropriately within their strategic decision-making process.

Human intelligence thrives on a rich tapestry of emotions and the ability for discernment, enabling individuals to experience and interpret the world in a profoundly complex manner. Emotions are not mere responses to stimuli; they are intricate processes that influence decision-making, creativity, empathy, and social interactions. The ability to feel joy, sorrow, love, and fear adds a layer of depth to human understanding that AI, in its current form, cannot grasp. Furthermore, emotional intelligence allows humans to navigate social complexities, build relationships, and make decisions that consider the well-being of others, aspects that algorithms and machine learning processes cannot authentically replicate.

Context is another cornerstone of human intelligence, encompassing the ability to understand the nuances of different situations and adjust behavior accordingly. Humans can discern subtle cues, such as cultural norms, body language, and the emotional state of others, to interpret situations with more sensitivity and understanding. This contextual awareness that comes naturally to humans enables a flexible and adaptive approach to problem-solving, compromise, and interaction, which AI struggles to emulate despite its ability to process and analyze data at an unprecedented scale. Ultimately, AI's interpretation of data is still confined to the parameters set by its creators and lacks the ability to perceive the intricacies of real-world scenarios beyond its programmed experience.

Deeply intertwined with emotion and context is judgment, or the capacity to make considered decisions. Human judgment involves weighing various factors, including ethical considerations, potential outcomes, and impact on others, to arrive at decisions that are not only logical but also morally sound. This aspect of human intelligence reflects the ability to think critically, reflect on past experiences, and project potential futures. AI, by its nature, is bound by algorithms and predictive models that rely solely on historical data. It simply lacks the capability to make value-based judgments or to understand the moral and ethical implications of its actions based not on what was, but what is and could be.

When it comes to the application of AI, this limitation also presents significant questions about who AI is made by, and ultimately for. The development and deployment of the technology has largely been driven by a field dominated by a specific demographic, which has inadvertently shaped the technology's perspective and constraints. The majority male-dominated culture within the tech industry has implications for the design and functionality of AI systems, potentially embedding biases and narrowing the scope of AI's understanding and applicability. This highlights a critical gap in AI's ability to cater to a diverse and inclusive range of perspectives, experiences, and needs.

While it represents a monumental leap in technology's capacity to process information and automate tasks, AI falls short of replicating the essence of human intelligence that is critical to sound and ethical decision-making. Moreover, its reliance on past data means it operates with a retrospective view, lacking an understanding of the present moment's dynamic and ever-changing nature. This temporal disconnect further underscores the challenge AI faces in mirroring the depth of human intelligence, which seamlessly integrates past experiences with present awareness to navigate the complexities of life. As we continue to advance in our technological capabilities, it is imperative to recognize and value the unique aspects of human intelligence that shape our world in ways that technology alone cannot duplicate.

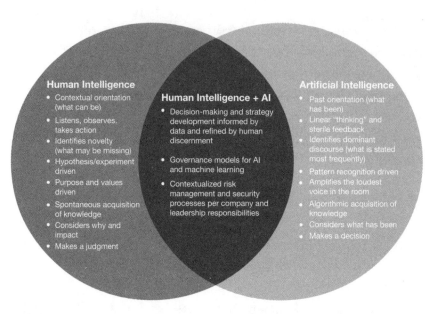

FIGURE 3.1 The unique and complementary skills of human and artificial intelligence.

It is also utterly important for businesses to capitalize on the benefits of when human and artificial intelligences work side by side (see Figure 3.1).

Our uniquely human abilities have heretofore been undervalued in the workplace and therefore our economy. But as workforce experts Aneesh Raman and Maria Flynn reflected in a 2024 article for the *New York Times*, "It's critical for us all to start from a place that imagines what's possible for humans in the age of A.I. When you do that, you find yourself focusing quickly on people skills that allow us to collaborate and innovate in ways technology can amplify but never replace."[2] As leaders, the opportunity for technological advances to positively reshape the way we work is dependent on our ability to reframe and invest in human intelligence as a complementary and equally valuable resource to AI. We must demonstrate this through a willingness and enthusiasm to upskill the workforce to keep pace with the change, and by centering humans in our approach for leveraging innovation.

Centering Humans in the Digital Age

In this new economic era, a key responsibility of leadership will be to leverage human intelligence and integrate it with technology for the benefit of both people and business. There's no getting around that AI will in fact disrupt the labor market, but as David Autor asserts, when applied well it can also "assist with restoring the middle-skill, middle-class heart of the U.S. labor market that has been hollowed out by automation and globalization."[3]

The leadership model of the future will be grounded in behaviors that help to develop human skills and create environments that promote human flourishing, despite and because of the increased role of AI. In other words, to stay ahead in the digital age, leaders will not only have to upskill workers, especially those considered gray-collar, but redefine what it means to engage a workforce with an increased say and growing expectations for leaders themselves.

Why? The pace of change and technological advancement, alongside global socioeconomic and political volatility, has given rise yet again to a new dynamic between employer and employee. It places more responsibility on leaders to help navigate the uncertainty by creating development and learning opportunities, promoting a sense of purpose and values, and establishing trust and stability within their own corporate culture. At the heart of all of this change is the imperative for leaders to lead differently. That is the only way they will acquire and retain the talent needed to meet the potential of the technology age, stay relevant in the market, and positively impact the world we live in.

We've often heard leaders talk about this idea that "what got us here will not get us where we need to go in business." These conversations usually involve talking about job descriptions, skills, and the capabilities of workers and potential employees as utilitarian – what the company needs from its people to get where it's going. Leading this way abandons the humanity of the workforce, and therefore the potential of an organization's most precious resource – its people. Instead, leaders must start asking: What do humans require of us?

This profound shift puts the responsibility on businesses to meet basic human needs, beyond a paycheck. It recognizes that for people to thrive, and ultimately contribute greatly to business, they require a different set of behaviors and mindsets from their leaders. From the board and CEO to those in the frontlines or on the "shopfloor," we must redefine how we think about people at work based on their essential needs for purpose, agency, connection, and well-being. These requirements are the foundation from which we all find stability, meaning, and motivation in our daily working lives, and they are the requirements around which to build a new leadership framework.

What Humans Require

CHAPTER

4

Purpose

"Never confuse movement with action."

—Ernest Hemingway[1]

Just as Maslow's Hierarchy of Needs outlines core requirements for human survival and motivation, people at work must have their needs met to flourish. To think of work as transactional – that employees achieve adequate satisfaction from a paycheck alone in return for labor – is outdated, and quite frankly illogical. We cannot simply check our humanity at the door of an office. It is only natural to find the same fundamental needs that drive us in the "real world" influencing how we operate and relate at work. And while previous generations were forced to subjugate their own needs under command-and-control-style leadership, today's increasingly powerful workforce demands that they be met. What humans require of their organizations is nothing new but nevertheless profound; put simply, people need to know that they matter. As leaders, we achieve that by empowering our workforce with a sense of agency, building connection, supporting their wellness, and, as we'll discuss in this chapter, rallying around a sense of purpose.

Over the course of history, not only have our management practices and principles changed, but people and their relationship to work has changed, too. As Caitlin Duffy, research director at Gartner, points out, "The intent to leave or stay in a job is only one of the things that people are questioning as part of the larger human story we are living.. . .You could call it the 'Great Reflection.'. . .It's critical to deliver value and purpose."[2]

In a volatile, post-pandemic world, many have found themselves reevaluating their priorities, asking themselves how they want to spend their time, what their values are, and what brings them a sense of satisfaction or fulfillment. Workers are asking themselves the same questions when it comes to their employer. In fact, more than half of US employees would be willing to take a pay cut to work at a company that shares their values, and 56% would not consider a job at a company whose values do not align with their own.[3] Moreover, Gallup research shows that with just a 10% improvement in employees' sense of connection to the mission or purpose of an organization, there is an 8.1% decrease in turnover and a 4.4% increase in profitability.[4]

Evidence of cultural change and workforce performance data make a clear case for reexamining the way that we engage people. In a world where workers have more choice and power than ever, we must shift the way we think about leveraging talent and optimizing performance. No longer is it enough to focus solely on what we require of people in terms of their skills and experience; rather, we must start asking ourselves what humans require of their organizations and leadership to grow, find satisfaction, and ultimately contribute to a company's purpose and success. As Jake Herway, the former culture transformation lead for Gallup, explained, "Organizational purpose becomes personal when the employee recognizes that their unique contribution furthers that goal."[5] But what does purpose mean in the context of work, and how do we reconcile the needs of an organization with those of the teams and individuals therein?

Defining Purpose: For What and for Whom Is All of This Meant?

For a company to have a clear sense of purpose, its daily work must be inspired by a set of values or guiding principles that answer this question: Why? Purpose provides a unifying story of how an organization and its people strive to make an impact – on both its external stakeholders and its internal community. It's what we should turn to as leaders, teams, and individual contributors when making decisions, big or small, and it becomes especially important as a guidepost in moments of great change or hardship.

As a company's various stakeholders become more aware, critical, and invested in how it communicates and abides by its values, important questions emerge about how to prioritize the needs and demands of various stakeholder groups on the way to reaching business goals. Leaders with a clear and strong understanding of purpose will be able to acknowledge and hold the tension of all voices – those of investors, consumers, workers, and our larger society – to the benefit of their business and their brand. Leaders who stray from their stated purpose and values for short-term gain risk the reputation and credibility of their brand as they become exposed in increasingly public forums. In the age of internet virality, the adage "any press is good press" is a PR fallacy.

Chevron and its CEO and chairman, Mike Wirth, stand out as a powerful example of a purpose-led leader and organization.

Now it may be odd to you that we start this discussion with an energy company, given the strong feelings many have about this industry. However, Mike Wirth's commitment to managing the interests of his shareholders and the oil-and-gas industry with those of environmentalists and a public increasingly interested in renewable energy is exactly what makes it worthwhile. As CEO and chairman, Wirth finds himself pushed to articulate Chevron's values more directly to speak to both the current reality and the demands of investors, consumers, activists, and government for how we source our energy in the future. "I'm not sure we are going to see a return to the days when CEOs did not speak out on issues," Wirth told CNBC. Still, given the company's global status, he noted, "You have to be thoughtful on the issues you do choose to really engage on."[6]

Chevron's purpose is documented in what's known as "The Chevron Way," which, as Wirth explains, "provides a foundation for what we value, what we believe and how we behave." Noted in the manifesto are both its stance on the future of energy being lower carbon, and its workplace values, including a culture built on trust, respect, and humility.[7] In action, Wirth has been a vocal spokesperson for the energy industry when it comes to the need for investment in renewable alternatives to petroleum. While reassuring ESG-centric investors that he will continue to explore new technologies that further their interests, he manages expectations with honesty: "This is not a cliff that will occur abruptly, this will be an evolution more than a revolution."

But, as evidenced in "The Chevron Way," Wirth's commitment goes beyond his investors and consumers. As the top leader of a large, multinational workforce, he is also keenly aware of the importance of a third stakeholder group: his employees. He explains, "If we were to be excused from the effort [for clean energy] by investors, we are missing an opportunity to engage some of the most talented and capable people on the planet.

I think that would be a mistake."[8] With a public commitment to develop "affordable, reliable, ever-cleaner energy that enables human progress" and a culture where "performance, truth and accountability guide the way," Wirth recognizes that the future of Chevron ultimately depends on and is driven by its ability to leverage and motivate human talent, contribution, and intelligence toward a shared vision.[9]

Let us now consider Patagonia, arguably on the opposite end of the spectrum of Chevron in many ways, though another fascinating example of the commitment to purpose-led leadership. Not only is the outdoor apparel brand environmentally conscious, but they are activists living their values out loud: in 2022, Patagonia's CEO, Yvon Chouinard, famously donated the company, valued at around $3 billion, to a specially designed trust and nonprofit organization that ensures all profits are used to fight climate change and protect undeveloped land around the world.[10] As is evidenced by this unprecedented move, their work on environmental issues has long been prioritized, even over the marketing of their products. Corley Kenna, Patagonia's director of global communications and public relations, noted that this purpose-led approach is not only good for the planet, but also for business. She told *Forbes* in 2019, "For us, it's more important to get the environmental story out than Patagonia the brand. ... We've found that when we put the planet first and do the right things for the planet, it winds up being good for business. It has proven itself over and over again."[11] In 2011, when Patagonia printed a Black Friday ad in the *New York Times* that read "Do not Buy This Jacket" in an effort to combat consumerism, sales increased by 30%. Although not the intended goal of the campaign, it simultaneously raised awareness for a growing problem.[12]

Moreover, Patagonia lives its values from the inside out. In reflecting on how other brands might start to build purpose into

their business, Kenna notes: "Before tackling brand transformation, you start by looking internally. How are your employees
treated? What are your company values? Do you have full visibility into the issues at hand?"[13] Chouinard has famously said
that he has run Patagonia like it will be around a hundred years
from now – and if we look at Patagonia's playbook, it would seem
that their path to ensuring that outcome is not only to invest in
the planet, but in the people who make the business possible.
In an interview with McKinsey, he gives credit to his workforce
for Patagonia's success: "The average lifespan of a corporation
currently is a little over 20 years, but we are still here after five
decades of doing things on our own terms. I'm proud of our
employees for getting us to this point."[14]

It's not a coincidence that Patagonia's workforce has achieved
such great success for the brand. The company has built a culture around integrity, transparency, flexibility, and inclusivity.
In his book *Let My People Go Surfing*, Chouinard outlines his
very human approach to leadership, in which employees are able
to take advantage of flexible hours to tend to childcare, pursue
education, or simply enjoy the great outdoors.[15] They're even
encouraged to participate in peaceful environmental protests,
for which the company will bail them out, pay for legal fees,
and compensate time away from work, if arrested. In terms of
employee engagement and performance, his policies seem to be
working. Patagonia boasts a 4% turnover rate, and Chief Human
Resources Officer Dean Carter has quipped that he does not keep
measuring employee engagement because it's not important to
know if employees are "97 percent or 98 percent engaged."[16]

It's not that Chouinard is not concerned about profit. He's
realistic that to achieve his and the company's purpose-driven
goals, it must meet financial targets. He writes in his book, "Our
mission statement says nothing about making a profit. In fact,
Malinda and I consider our bottom line to be the amount of

good that the business has accomplished over the year. However, a company needs to be profitable in order to stay in business and to accomplish all its other goals, and we do consider profit to be a vote of confidence that our customers approve of what we are doing."[17] Chouinard's leadership of Patagonia is a masterclass in delivering stakeholder value around a clear and actionable purpose – in his case, for the good of the planet and its people.

Through Chevron and Patagonia, we see how purpose is defined and played out within two seemingly disparate corporations and industries. Their leaders navigate diverse stakeholder interests and generate value for them not by pandering to each of their needs mindlessly, but through honesty, transparency, pragmatism, and a sharp focus on carrying out their organization's "why" in all decision-making. The answer to that fundamental question comes to life in the companies' service and product offering as much as it does in their leadership philosophy and culture. In a stakeholder-driven economy, these examples demonstrate how a successful organization's "why" is always at the heart of its "how."

Purpose Washing, Virtue Signaling, and the Pitfalls of Disingenuous Leadership

In a world where war, climate change, political instability, inflation, and issues like racial and reproductive justice and gun control dominate the news cycle, consumers have become increasingly concerned with their role in supporting businesses that align with their values. In fact, 62% of consumers want companies to stand up for the issues they care about, and 66% believe that transparency is one of a brand's most attractive qualities.[18] Product quality and utility alone no longer cut it when it comes to a customer's purchasing behavior; often they care as much about the impact a brand is making as they do about their offering.

Knowing this, many brands have been quick to update their marketing strategy to include messaging around purpose and values. And therein lies the problem: It is one thing to think about your mission statement with the consumer and other stakeholders in mind to inform and guide how you'll do business; after all, the whole point of being purpose-driven is to evaluate how your work can and will make an impact on others. But it is another thing entirely to define your purpose by calculating which messaging will prove more profitable than another solely from a marketing perspective. With this mindset, an organization is at risk of adjusting their purpose as they would their sails with the wind – and their brand will be quickly exposed as fickle and untrustworthy by the very consumers they hoped to woo with their loud but superficial sense of purpose.

With social media as a rapidly growing and increasingly important marketing channel for brands, we also see countless cases of disingenuous leadership played out on social media in response to social movements or cultural moments. These tactics are used to gain credibility with stakeholders without any real depth or follow-through. Especially since 2020, in the wake of the global pandemic, George Floyd's murder, and the overturning of *Roe v. Wade*, brands have been under pressure to meet the moment and take responsibility for their role in effecting social change. To be fair, it is an incredibly complicated sociopolitical landscape for leaders to navigate and it's fair to expect that even with good intentions, mistakes will be made. But in many ways, it's also simple. If your instinct is to speak up on an issue in the news cycle publicly, you must also ask: Are these values I'm promoting being lived out within my organization already? Is there something more we could be doing to further this cause that aligns with our purpose? Am I ready and willing to be accountable for any blind spots or missteps I make along the way?

How can I learn more about this issue so that we as an organization can do better for our people?

In June 2020, millions of Instagram users posted black squares to their feeds for #BlackoutTuesday to express solidarity with the Black Lives Matter movement. Over 950 brands participated, but as popularity of the hashtag rose, so did criticism of the initiative for being performative and shallow – many posted the square with only the hashtag in the caption or a couple of short lines to express allyship. The tens of millions of posts ultimately drowned out Black voices central to the movement and sharing critical information and updates about the latest news, protests, and donation links.[19] Of those who posted the black square that day, many individuals and companies ended up taking theirs down, offering apology for the short-sightedness of their quick reaction to the trend.

As discussion of anti-racism took center stage, consumers started to expect more of the brands they supported, especially if they touted DEI (diversity, equity, inclusion) efforts on their websites. In a survey conducted by Edelman in 2020, 60% of American respondents said they expected brands to utilize marketing dollars to advocate for racial equality. In response to these findings, Edelman CEO Richard Edelman remarked, "Brands are now being pushed to go beyond their classic business interests to become advocates. It is a new relationship between company and consumer, where purchase is premised on the brand's willingness to live its values, act with purpose, and if necessary, make the leap into activism."[20]

Companies that demonstrated a tangible commitment in the fight for racial justice emerged from this challenging moment with increased credibility and respect, even if they too had initially fumbled by posting a square on #BlackoutTuesday or faced criticism in the past for racist discrimination. Take Sephora, which, having fit both criteria, subsequently closed all its retail stores for two hours for employees to attend company-wide racial bias training. Their US business also became the first major retailer to sign on to the 15% pledge, a campaign founded by Aurora James asking retailers to dedicate 15% of their shelf space to Black-owned businesses (approximately proportional to the Black population in the US).[21]

Employees were likewise auditing their employers for evidence that their values were being lived out internally. In 2020, the makeup brand Glossier was called out for the disparity between their outward displays of diversity and the company's internal reality. At the time, the brand, which had presented itself as inclusive and forward-thinking in its marketing, spoke out in support of the Black Lives Matter movement and donated $1 million to Black-owned beauty businesses and organizations working on racial justice initiatives through a new grant initiative. Meanwhile, inside the organization, employees had a different experience. A collective of former retail employees called "Outta the Gloss" penned an open letter to Glossier on Instagram that August, exposing a "sometimes racist and inequitable working environment" and called for a boycott of the brand. Glossier's failure to respond in a meaningful way to employee demands ultimately left consumers disillusioned by the beauty favorite. In 2021, they renewed their grant program "as part of a broader $10 million commitment to bolster equity, inclusion, and representation in the beauty industry over the next five years."[22]

On the other end of the spectrum, in a profound demonstration of aligning word and action Mastercard announced their Solidarity Initiative in September 2020, a $500 million investment into Black communities, which acknowledged the economic vulnerability that Black people face amid racial inequity, on top of those resulting from COVID-19 and the risks they face from police brutality.[23] The focus of the initiative, which invested in Black businesses and aimed to make financial tools and resources more affordable and accessible, also looked inward at their own workforce and made a promise to enhance their "end-to-end talent program to ensure we are recruiting, developing and retaining Black employees at every level." These commitments included partnering with historically Black colleges and universities for recruitment, growing Black leadership at the VP-level and above by 50%, investing in formal training and mentorship for Black colleagues, and increasing transparency on the progress toward these goals.[24]

Two years later, in June 2022, the US faced another pivotal turning point for equality when *Roe v. Wade* was overturned by the Supreme Court, and leaders were challenged with a new set of values-driven questions. With access to abortion at risk in many states, employers were now forced to ask themselves what their role was in supporting their workforce's access to reproductive care, especially if the company was based in one of the 13 states with measures in place to immediately ban or severely limit abortion access. Many were quick to update their HR policies to include stipends for traveling out of state for abortion care, relocation reimbursements, and other abortion care benefits.[25] And in recognition that many of those most affected by this decision do not work at an organization like their own, several brands made donations to various abortion funds or reproductive rights organizations, and called for others to do the same and take a stand. Levi Strauss issued this statement: "Protection of reproductive rights is a critical business issue impacting our workforce, our economy and progress toward gender and racial equity. Given what is at stake, business leaders need to make their voices heard."[26]

These examples certainly demonstrate how companies have taken on a larger role and an increased sense of responsibility in advocating for social change and justice, and demonstrating lived values internally, especially in response to major events.

But we'd argue that purpose washing and virtue signaling are most pervasive and insidious when it comes to business as usual. Many organizations flaunt fancy "about us" pages that state lofty values and a commitment to diversity, equity, and inclusion, and highlight their wellness, sustainability, or charitable programs and initiatives. For companies whose actions align with their words, the promotion of these efforts is a fantastic way to attract talent and appeal to like-minded consumers. But far too often we see something else happening: employees joining a company due to a perceived shared passion and belief system, only to leave disillusioned and disappointed by their lived experience within the organization. We see this when companies inflate their commitment to these ideals because of optics, or when – with best intention – they overpromise and try to be everything to everyone.

As a company working toward its business goals, the latter is impossible. But in today's sociopolitical climate and changing workforce culture, it has become increasingly challenging to know when to leverage your company's voice and resources to speak up on issues publicly or take a stand internally. When it comes to advocacy and social change, how do leaders know where corporate accountability ends and individual responsibility begins? The truth is, it's not always cut and dried – we are asking these questions because we have been faced with unprecedented challenges and significant cultural shifts that do not come with a playbook. Take, for example, divisive issues such as the Israel-Hamas war, or the dilemma companies were faced with during the height of the pandemic with whether to enforce a COVID-19 vaccine policy. Circumstances like these have left even the most seasoned leaders and their employees confused and anxious about how to proceed.

In this environment, a clearly defined purpose and set of lived values are an organization's superpower. Effective leaders use these as tools against which to weigh any issue by asking whether addressing it is imperative to carrying out the company's purpose, or if it otherwise calls upon the values-driven commitments it's made to its people (as related to DEI, health and well-being, or human rights, for example). If the answer is yes, leaders must evaluate what lies within their organization's power and resources to respond or repair meaningfully – first and foremost with their team before speaking publicly. And most importantly, they must communicate with honesty and compassion, no matter what the conclusion is. Leaders cannot expect that ignoring an issue will make it go away. In a world overflowing with spin and shine, winning the trust and buy-in of stakeholders comes down to integrity.

Purpose and Values Take Center Stage

Honesty and integrity are especially critical for engaging the Gen Z workforce, who, having grown up in the aftermath of 9/11, wars in the Middle East, the Great Recession, a global pandemic, racial unrest, and a government insurrection, find themselves skeptical of authority and the institutions that are supposed to keep them safe and spur progress. In an interview with the *Washington Post*, one young worker reflected, "What's important for me is that not only am I a fit for the job but is the job a fit for me. The makeup of the organization is important to me almost as much as the work I'm going to be doing."[27] This generation knows that in a tightening labor market, they have options when it comes to where and how they apply their skills. They expect more transparency, honesty, and integrity from their employers, and have little tolerance for lip service. This is a generation of realists. And while they have certain ideals – namely when it comes to work–life balance, the environment, and equality – they would rather be told the truth about the status quo than get caught in a corporate honey trap.

On the other end of the generational divide, we find Baby Boomers and late Gen Xers at the end of their careers with a growing interest in the idea of purpose and values in the context of their legacy. Known historically to be work-centric, competitive, and conservative, this generation now finds itself prioritizing the "heart side" of business after years of considering first and foremost their fiduciary responsibility.[28] For this group, legacy is rarely about more volume or revenue; it centers around their impact on people. For some, it's too little, too late. But for many others, there is ample time and opportunity to make a difference in their last working chapter. In fact, workers over 75 are the fastest-growing age group in the workforce,[29] and just like their younger counterparts, some of these workers are now facing a shift in mindset and priorities. After years of toeing the company line, these last years are defined by mentorship and stewardship in preparing the next generation to take the wheel. This fascinating development means that now, both the youngest and some of the oldest participants in our workforce are placing a growing importance on purpose, values, and people in their workplace.

Building Purpose

The true impact of a purpose-led business model is only fully realized when an entire organization, from individual contributors to the C-suite and board, are aligned and clear on their mission-driven priorities and values. It's important to employees to feel a sense of purpose at work; in fact, 70% of respondents in a McKinsey study reported that their sense of purpose is largely defined by work. And yet 85% of those employees say that they are unsure or disagree that they are able to live their purpose in their daily work, as compared to 85% of executives and upper management who say they can. The "purpose gap" that this study reveals is profound – less-satisfied workers reported struggling with lower energy, lower engagement, and less excitement about work, which, as the research points out "inevitably translate[s] to negative outcomes for the business."[30] If executives fail to understand the realities and motivations of their workforce, they will fail to find and leverage the talent needed to meet their objectives.

So how does leadership instill a sense of purpose from the ground up? Let us return to the concept of power skills. Leaders must adopt a new mindset and be trained with the relevant capabilities to engage and motivate people. That means being intentional with time spent in one-on-ones and team meetings to better understand the individuals who drive work forward and how they can uniquely contribute to carrying out that purpose. It means modeling purpose-driven decision-making and saying no to the initiatives and ideas that distract from making impact according to that purpose. And it means assessing performance and how work gets done against the values an organization espouses outwardly.

At Johnson & Johnson, the company's credo is quite literally carved in stone at the entrance of the headquarters in New Brunswick, New Jersey. In brief, it makes a commitment to put the well-being and health of the people they serve first – that includes healthcare workers, patients, and parents, as well as their employees, shareholders, and the environment.[31] It was one of the first of its kind that spoke to corporate social responsibility and that put the needs of people first.[32] For J&J, it's "more than just a moral compass. . .it's a recipe for business success" that has served their organization well for over a hundred years.[33]

When asked about the companies' longevity, J&J's chief historian, Margaret Gurowitz, reflected, "One of the reasons for that success has been a willingness to embrace change – without changing the values of the credo." Of course, over the years, the brand has made some updates to modernize it, including calling for an inclusive work environment – but the essence of its pledge has remained true and central to its business operations through change, disruption, and challenges over the course of more than a century.[34]

As we have seen through this example and many others, a sense of purpose is what sustains, orients, and motivates people through the highs and lows of their working lives. It carries us through the unknown, the grueling, the boring, and the difficult. It reminds us not only of what's right and what matters, but of what all our striving is for. Without purpose, it becomes nearly impossible to harness the focus, determination, and tenacity required to innovate and make an impact in a world as ripe with roadblocks as it is with opportunity. As our culture continues to evolve toward an increased demand for corporate social responsibility, a company's earnest commitment to purpose and values is how it will stand out to consumers, workers, and shareholders alike.

CHAPTER

5

Agency

"Claim your power, and bring along your full humanity. Clear the way for others to do the same. Because what our families, our companies, and the world needs is nothing more – and nothing less – than exactly who we are."

—Abby Wambach, *Wolfpack*[1]

More than ever, people are seeking out purpose-driven work that aligns with the cross-section of their interests and values. For companies, it is the foundation by which they and their leaders build relationships with stakeholders. As purpose becomes ever more critical to the success of a business and the satisfaction of people who work there, we see an increased desire from the workforce to take ownership of their contribution to an organization's broader mission. With clarity of purpose and the freedom to make decisions around how they approach tasks, manage projects, and solve problems, workers are likely to be more satisfied, committed, engaged, and trusting of their employers.

For too long, though, workers have felt that they lack a voice within their company's stakeholder matrix – that they operate without agency to influence how their company does business, from their environmental impact and sociopolitical affiliations to their partnerships and internal policies and strategy. But workers will no longer allow for these decisions that ultimately impact the way we all work, live, shape our futures, and fulfill our purpose, to stay in the hands of a few at the top of their organizations. And neither should leaders; it is in every organization's interest to leverage the passions and interests of their people to innovate and expand the influence and impact of their work. True leadership recognizes that when we empower people with opportunities to take ownership and enable their agency, it's a win-win for workers and business.

Unfortunately, the workforce's demand for a voice has too often been met with patchwork solutions from employers like perfunctory employee sentiment surveys that, without meaningful follow-through, fail to address the underlying causes of low engagement. At worst, they misuse AI-enabled platforms to scrape employee emails, analyze their behaviors on video, and ultimately erode trust via Big Brother tactics in the name of understanding their people better. The result of these efforts is almost always the opposite of what their workers actually require: Without a voice to contribute or influence meaningfully, workers become disillusioned by the lack of action from employers and, in the case of invasive monitoring, disengage altogether to protect themselves within a culture of fear.

In the modern workforce, we are not only witnessing a demand for increased agency on the individual level; we also see this trend on the collective and community levels. People are aware, like we have never seen before in our lifetimes, of the power of their voice – and they are simply not willing to work or participate in society without the ability to use it and exercise autonomy in how they work and live. And yet, only 17% of workers report that their business is very ready to address an increase in worker influence and choice.[2] We'd argue that this is because leaders are still stuck in the mindset of what they require from workers, rather than prioritizing what humans require of them: an environment that creates opportunity for and empowers people to exercise their agency in pursuit of their purpose.

Individual Agency: Where, When, and How We Work

Workers today seek more control in where, when, and how they work. Especially since 2020 when most office workers were sent home to work remotely, there has been a shift in thinking in respect to workplace flexibility. Mass exposure to how distributed work could function opened up possibilities and opportunities for many, who until that point may not have realized that there was another way for work to get done outside of a nine-to-five, in-office framework. Without a commute, fixed hours away from home, or even the need to adhere to the standards for business attire, time and space became available that allowed work to fit into our lives, and not the other way around. That's not to say that our time spent in lockdown was easy or that remote work is a perfect solution for all businesses. But the shared experience did expose us to a new idea: Increased flexibility in how, when, and where we work ultimately provides us more choice and autonomy.

As it turns out, having a sense of autonomy is one of the most important intrinsic drivers of threat and reward in the brain.[3] This is why we see such strong reactions and disengagement when faced with in-office mandates or cultures based on a command-and-control-style leadership – our aversion to not having a say is hard-wired in our brains. In fact, 59% of workers report that they would not work for a company requiring them to be in the office five days a week. When Apple announced that employees must return to the office just three days a week, the company faced multiple resignations and an open letter from employees stating they felt 'not just unheard, but at times actively ignored." Central to their demands was that teams have as much autonomy in their decisions around remote or location-flexible work as they have in their hiring decisions.[4]

Decisions around working models must always consider this threat to individual autonomy if the policies are to be accepted and successful. We have far too often seen the effects of arbitrary return-to-office mandates that do not take into consideration the human requirements and realities that shape a worker's ability to show up fully. Take Dell, for example, which in 2024 issued a return-to-office mandate after a decade of modeling a forward-looking hybrid working model that allowed employees to grow their careers even as they navigated life changes and circumstances such as having a disability, welcoming children, or taking care of an elderly parent. Under the new policy, remote workers would no longer be eligible for promotion or role change. In the wake of the announcement, Dell faced harsh criticism and backlash from employees and the public, with one senior team member observing, "Every team I work with has at least one person if not two or three affected by this policy. They are overwhelmingly women. This new policy on its face appears to be anti-remote, but in practice will be anti-woman."[5]

In this example, we see how a company's values are inextricably linked to their employees' ability to exercise agency. The fact that women are disproportionately affected by return-to-office mandates exposes the lack of consideration employers have for accommodating and advocating for the needs of its workers. In this case, women, who make up the majority of our society's caregivers, are once again faced with a roadblock to their career development as a direct result of not having a choice in where, how, and when they work.

On the flipside, we see employers like Sanofi put their values into action by guaranteeing workers one year of salary and social and emotional support after a cancer diagnosis. Furthermore, the company promises that employees will be able to "incorporate further flexible work arrangements to better navigate cancer and work."[6] This policy not only provides psychological safety to workers during an uncertain time, but it also actively encourages them to exercise their agency in how they approach treatment alongside their career. As Sanofi's chief people officer points out, "The last thing you want to be thinking about when you are diagnosed with cancer, or going through treatment, is work." Through this program, Sanofi replaces an employee's fear of repercussions with the reassurance that their role as an employer is to support that individual's decisions – first around treatment, and then around work.

The Privilege of "Whole Self"

In 1985, psychologists Richard Ryan and Edward Deci developed their self-determination theory, which identifies autonomy as a key component of intrinsic human motivation and asserts that for people to feel a sense of personal empowerment, they must be the "causal agent of their own lives."[7] In the workplace, this idea not only pertains to where, how, and when we work. The concept of self-determination extends in no small measure to defining our own identity within the context of our workplace; it is about the agency to decide how we show up and which parts of ourselves we share with the world.

In the 2010s, a popular management trend was to encourage people to bring their "whole selves" to work. The thought behind this idea is a good one, but as we know, intention does not supersede impact, and the ability to bring your "whole self" to work is in fact a great privilege. For marginalized groups especially, sharing everything with an employer and with colleagues can be risky, if not dangerous, and the concept is therefore laced with fear, anxiety, and legitimate concerns of bias and discrimination around personal information that is not legally protected. In practice, the instruction to bring your "whole self" to work results in the opposite outcome than what was intended. It increases the rate of "covering" in the workplace, or the act of hiding our true selves by blending in and downplaying our differences to avoid judgment and discrimination.

In 2013, Christie partnered with Kenji Yoshino to study the impact of covering and found that 61% of people were covering some part of themselves at work, whether their sexuality, ethnicity, family structure, or mental health, and that it had a significant impact on their sense of self. Ten years later, Dr. Yoshino revisited the study with Deloitte and the Meltzer Center for Diversity, Inclusion, and Belonging at NYU School of Law, and found that despite increased efforts toward DEI, covering still remains a concerning issue in our workforce today, with 60% of respondents reporting covering in the last 12 months.[8] In a post-pandemic world, where work has literally infiltrated our homes, the right to privacy and choice around the parts of ourselves that we share with others remains critical – especially so long as leaders fail to create psychologically safe environments for their people.

The truth is that work is historically an area where humans have had little agency. In hierarchical structures run by "hero" leaders who call the shots, workers have been expected to adhere to the rules and directives from above with little pushback, lest they be labeled "not a team player." But every individual should have absolute agency over what personal information they share with their colleagues, and leaders must work to create environments in which that choice is encouraged and respected.

Over the last 50 years, however, our promises for diversity, equity, and inclusion have largely failed to result in representation in the executive ranks. We have not been successful at creating spaces and cultures where people of color, the LGBTQIA2+ community, people with disabilities, and women feel safe, seen, and valued. Take employee resource groups (ERGs), for example. The original concept was that people of similar backgrounds and with similar experiences in the world could support each other in rising through corporate culture – but when we look at the pipeline of women and people of color moving up the corporate ladder, it's clear that the promise of fulfilling DEI commitments through employee-run programs like ERGs and other education initiatives has not come to fruition. While women in the C-suite increased from 17% to 28% between 2015 and 2023, only 6% of that group are women of color. Moreover, women in director-level positions are leaving the workforce at higher rates than in past years, especially as compared to their male counterparts.[9] The challenges we have faced in achieving results through DEI initiatives are not a result or reflection of the quality of these programs themselves necessarily; they are the result of the way we have thought about management and the active role leaders play in ensuring equal representation throughout, and especially at the top, of their organizations.

The pitfall of many companies and their management is that a vastly white, male leadership demographic does not receive enough training, education, and exposure to collaboration with a diverse set of peers to recognize and avoid bias. As a result of this bias, workers often end up being defined by a single attribute that is incredibly limited and laced with an undercurrent of prejudice, whether of age, gender, race, or sexual orientation. This is at the root of why people of color, women, and especially women of color, have yet to reach the top of our organizations in meaningful numbers or be paid equally for equal work. Our failure to address the systemic bias and discrimination that prevents true diversity and representation from penetrating the C-suite is shameful, and it reveals a deeply concerning truth: At the most basic level, we have denied people, especially the marginalized, the agency to define themselves in their own words and not by the constructs of society and those in power in their workplace.

Taking Ownership of Our Identity

Michele Norris is an American journalist and founder of the Race Card Project, an initiative focused on creating conversation around identity to combat the reductive labels and stereotypes thrust upon each other in the absence of real connection or understanding. As she wrote for an article about the project in the *Washington Post*, "I have always cringed when the accusations fly about someone allegedly 'playing the race card.' It's usually a proxy for 'You're making me uncomfortable, so please stop talking'. . .so, in 2010, I flipped the script, turning that accusatory phrase into a prompt to spark conversation." To start, she printed 200 black postcards with simple instructions: "Race. Your thoughts. Six words. Please send." and left them everywhere she traveled. She has received over 500,000 six-word stories since, and has expanded her initiative online, where people can engage around each other's words. As Norris notes, the stories have "sparked hundreds of conversations that, little by little, help broaden people's understanding about difference and identity."[10]

Inspired by Norris's work, a major international tech company introduced a new initiative to its teams called "You in 6 Words" to embolden employees with a pathway for defining who they are, not what they are, with their colleagues. Choosing their own words allowed them to celebrate the parts of themselves they felt comfortable sharing within the walls of the workplace, sometimes informed by but very often beyond their racial, gender, or sexual identity. The process was built on an underlying belief that we are all multidimensional, with stories far more complex than our public personas or "labels" can capture. It built bridges across differences and connected teams around a better and shared understanding of each other and themselves. By encouraging a simple act of storytelling, the company's leadership transferred a sense of ownership, power, and meaningful connection to its workforce that would carry through to the way they worked individually and collaborated with one another toward a shared goal.

Empowering individual agency is in fact the key to systemic change. When people can define themselves outside of the burden of cultural and societal constructs, they are instilled with a sense of worth and value that cannot be accessed fully otherwise in the workplace. As a result, they show up to meetings, one-on-ones, and their own work with a sense of power and the motivation for productivity and progress. Rather than forcing people into a defensive position of seeking validation and acceptance to survive unfair circumstances, agency empowers people to push forward for the mutual benefit of themselves and the company they work for on terms they drafted. And as they do, the ability for their leaders and peers to see each person in all of their individuality and humanity expands, compounds, and improves conditions for all.

Collective Agency: The Rise of Unions Brings Us Back to the Future

In 2023, the number of workers who walked off the job increased by 141% from the year before.[11] The year brought with it big strides for labor unions with strikes against the likes of SAG-AFTRA, Ford, GM, and across sectors from healthcare to hotels and casinos. MIT professor and unionization expert Thomas Kochan coined the term the "Great Reset" to reflect "the big wage settlements, the threat of strikes, [and] the use of the strike as a source of power way above anything that has been achieved since the early 2000s."[12] The number of high-profile strikes in recent years is particularly remarkable considering that US labor laws present significant obstacles to unions, its members, and those who would like to join. In a growing stakeholder economy, however, the workforce, even in the US, has become increasingly aware of how formidable they can be when they lock arms – and the resurgence of unions is a powerful demonstration of that collective agency.

It's interesting to note that while the absolute number of workers in unions has increased in recent years, the percentage of unionized workers within the workforce overall has in fact declined; the creation of new non-union jobs has simply outpaced unionized roles in the marketplace.[13] And yet 54% of Americans say that the decline of unions over past decades has been bad for the country, and 59% report that the trend is particularly bad for working people.[14] There's truth to this belief. Workers covered by a union contract earn 10.2% more in wages than their non-union counterparts. The difference is even larger when we look at marginalized groups. Black workers earn 13.1% more than their non-union peers, while Hispanic workers are paid 18.8% more on average. Historically, unions have not only played a large role in helping close wage gaps for Black and Hispanic workers, but they have also helped to improve the health and safety of the workforce by guaranteeing sick leave, health insurance, and the enforcement of safety protocols. With the decline of unions and the introduction of laws to weaken them over the past four decades, we have seen the pay gap between white and Black workers widen, as well as an increase in the rate of occupational fatalities.[15]

The mindset around collective action and strikes in the US differs significantly from Europe, where there is a strong and active culture of collective bargaining. Here, instead of the burden being placed on workers to organize within their companies or industries, labor laws empower them to unionize across entire sectors of the economy and classes of workers.[16] Considering that the path to collective action is not only clearer, it's endorsed by its governments and the broader culture, it's no surprise that Europeans have a higher rate of unionized workers than the US. A 2009 article in the *New York Times* exploring the historical context of the differences between European and American attitudes toward strikes opined, "Today, American workers, even those earning $20,000 a year, tend to view themselves as part of an upwardly mobile middle class. In contrast, European workers often still see themselves as proletarians in an enduring class struggle."[17]

Today, Europeans on average work fewer hours than Americans, thanks in part to more paid holidays, shorter working weeks for full-time employees, and a larger share of part-time workers. The employment rate in the EU is higher than in the United States, and many countries report a similar productivity level per hour as their American counterparts; in fact, German workers are even 1% more productive per hour than US workers.[18] Is there a correlation between these facts and Europe's pro-union culture? History would suggest there is. Until the 1970s, French employees worked more hours than Americans. When the country was faced with rising unemployment, their solution came in the form of work sharing. Individuals with jobs would reduce their hours to increase employment opportunities for those without. Under the catchphrase "work less, work all," French unions advocated for this approach, which they argued would ultimately benefit society at large. The policy, which allowed everyone to work but with more time off, set a new standard within the culture for work–life balance, and ultimately strengthened the role of unions and solidified the role of collective bargaining within the country. Bruce Sacerdote, Dartmouth professor of economics and expert in workplace trends, noted, "France's policies are not making the country lazy. Instead, taking a liberal amount of time off – and fully disconnecting when they do so – tends to make people more productive during the hours they are actually on the clock."[19]

History proves, both in the US and in Europe, that unions play a critical role in protecting the interests of the collective in a way that ultimately benefits the individual. Even though within the US non-union jobs are growing at a faster rate than unionized roles and with the barriers that the legal system presents, there seems to be a clear appetite within society for leveraging its collective voice to achieve better working conditions, protect the interests of workers, and use a shared voice to influence the future of business. Public approval of labor unions is at its highest since 1965 in the US, and election petitions to form unions are increasing, with a 53% jump between 2021 and 2022.[20] The increase in the number of strikes in recent years and media coverage of high-profile walkouts have only increased interest in collective action – so much so that Americans believe, more than ever in recent history, that labor unions will become stronger. And as unions and the right to strike gain wider public support, striking workers become more powerful when it comes time to negotiate with employers eager to avoid a PR disaster.[21]

In our digital world, workers can leverage the court of public opinion more than ever to give weight to their demands. In 2023, 1500 employees at Google, supported by unions such as the Alphabet Workers Union, United Tech, and Allied Workers, penned an open letter to Alphabet's CEO to call attention to the global impact of the company's recent layoffs. The letter outlined several demands, including asking for voluntary layoffs before mandatory ones, allowing people to finish paid time off, especially paternity and bereavement leave, and to consider forgoing layoffs of those in places around the world facing humanitarian crisis.[22] The petition, in essence, centered around making the process of downsizing more humane.

Even without the backing of unions, workers today can and will use their collective voice to speak truth to power. In the wake of ChatGPT's founder Sam Altman being fired by the board, 730 workers signed an open letter demanding his reinstatement and the resignation of the board. The letter read, "The process through which you terminated Sam Altman and removed Greg Brockman from the board has jeopardized all this work and undermined our mission and company. Your conduct has made it clear you did not have the competence to oversee OpenAI."[23] Only days after he was fired and the open letter was sent, Sam Altman was reinstated as CEO.

The role of unions has always been critical in advocating for the interests of frontline workers, ultimately giving them a voice in the C-suite and ensuring fair pay, treatment, and protection under the law. Their role has been especially important for marginalized groups, including blue-collar workers. Today, as we usher AI and other technological advancements into more workplaces, they could continue to play a pivotal role for the gray-collar workers whose livelihoods are under threat from automation without proper upskilling. Consider the Hollywood strikes in 2023, during which a crucial bargaining point was the protection of workers, especially those living paycheck to paycheck, from AI learning and then replacing their creative skillset to the benefit and cost savings of the studios. The strikes represented the first high-profile showdown between human workers and technology and ultimately served to increase interest from other industries in the role unions could play in protecting their jobs from the encroachment of technology.[24] For gray-collar workers, like for so many other groups, the ability to leverage their collective agency in the same way and advocate for their role in the workforce will be of paramount importance – not only for their individual well-being, but for that of the middle class and the future of the economy.

What's in the interest of workers is almost always in the interest of organizations. People who benefit from fair pay, proper healthcare coverage, and a right to personal time off and sick leave are more engaged and productive workers.[25] Consider that in the 17 American states with the highest union densities, wage gaps are significantly smaller, and workers are more likely to have access to health insurance, retirement plans, and paid leave. In these states, we even see increased government revenue and decreased spending. What's more, in states with a higher density of unions, we see increased civic engagement and political advocacy that benefits the broader community, especially around worker empowerment and economic justice issues.[26] By engaging with unions and working with groups advocating for improved policies and conditions, companies contribute to a more functional, healthier society – one that can focus on progress rather than on making ends meet. When the collective demands access to these basic needs, employers must rise to meet them. Their voices are only getting stronger.

Community Agency: Harnessing Purpose and Values to Effect Change

More than ever, we are witnessing demands for change happen at the community level with the power to impact the broader experience and well-being of workers, or groups of workers, regardless of their particular employer. Agency on the community level means that we as a society have a voice in the trajectory of our own futures, and that through community-based action, we are able to affect change that benefits everyone who works within our communities.

A benefit today of our digital-everything world is that it's easier than ever to learn about the strides and efforts others are making far away from our own homes. You may well remember the walkout in Iceland in 2023, during which many businesses across the country shut down when tens of thousands of women, including the prime minister, stopped work for a full day in protest of the gender pay gap and as a call to action against gender-based violence. With a clear message about the value of women's contribution to the workforce, the strike disrupted industries from public transportation and hospitality to healthcare and education.[27] Though we still have a long way to go in terms of closing the gender pay gap – at our current rate it will take 250 years[28] – the walkout generated global media attention on the issue of gender inequality and the $10.9 trillion value of women's unpaid labor.[29]

This event, which may have occurred thousands of miles away from your community, is certain to still have had an impact on it. Over the last decade, there has been a swell of news coverage and storytelling around women's experiences in the workplace and on income inequality between genders and races – and between races within genders. The #MeToo movement has resulted in powerful top executives being ousted from their seats and more than 80 workplace anti-harassment bills.[30] Moreover, it demonstrated to survivors the power of their voices when supported by a collective.

In 2022, the United States Congress passed the Speak Out Act to ban nondisclosure agreements in sexual harassment and assault cases, which had once been standard form in employment agreements and prohibited victims from speaking out, to anyone, about their own experience in the workplace. Of NDAs, Gretchen Carlson, co-founder of the advocacy group Lift Our Voices, "The point of NDAs is to cover up behavior, but it's also to stop the women from being able to coalesce together to realize that they are not the only one."[31] In other words, this type of NDA once served to eliminate the possibility for collective action – to take away women's agency. In the end, it was in fact women across a multitude of organizations, industries, and geographies who successfully worked together to bring about change, fueled by a shared experience in the workplace.

On the state level in the US, community-based action has also helped to bring about change in the form of pay transparency laws that ultimately empower workers to advocate for fair pay in the hiring process. These laws were born out of increased demand from a workforce growing increasingly frustrated with the uncertainty of whether their pay was on par with industry, geographical, and internal company benchmarks. Especially beneficial for women and people of color, pay transparency laws help to level the playing field of income inequality on the state level.[32] Culturally, this movement has resulted in candidates screening out job postings that do not publish a salary range as expectations mount for employers to offer more upfront data about how they value roles within their companies. As a result, more employers, even in states without these laws, are opting into publishing salaries voluntarily[33] – a move that may very well help recruiters find and retain a better match for their open positions.

The support of an organization for the causes their workforce and larger community care about can have a powerful impact on employee engagement and buy-in. Over the last year, we have seen companies endorse and empower their teams to attend protests with the likes of movements like #FridaysForFuture and #BlackLivesMatter. For workers who may already be supporting these causes in their private lives, the demonstration of cultural and contextual awareness and solidarity from an employer speaks loudly. In a study from Rice University on how institutional support of DEI affects a company's bottom line, they found that organizations where employees perceived high levels of support also reported higher revenue than companies whose employees did not feel that way. Of the study, co-author Mikki Hebl said, "By investing in the well-being of their employees and employees' communities, organizations can play a really important role in moving society closer to a world where everyone can thrive."[34] Here again, we see the power of purpose in the workplace. This time, it not only serves as a guide for how an organization, its leaders, and their teams operate; it also provides a meaningful foundation for empowering acts of agency on the community level for the mutual benefit of the people and businesses who work within it.

Modern Leaders Embrace Agency

Restaurateur and author of *Unreasonable Hospitality* Will Guidara is known for saying, "Adversity is a terrible thing to waste." Guidara has spoken often about the challenges of turning around a struggling business, and how critical it is for leaders to engage their team in finding the way out. According to him, there is power in sitting in the disappointment and frustration of adversity – to use it as fuel for finding innovative solutions. Guidara's philosophy is that through hard times and good, a leader's primary role is to communicate clearly on what needs to get done and why, and then to empower their employees to figure out how. In 2017, after years of uphill battles, 11 Madison Park became the world's number-one restaurant under Guidara's leadership.

Globally, only one in four workers strongly believes that their voice is valued at work.[35] And yet we know that employees who think that their opinions matter are 4.6 times more likely to feel empowered to do their best work.[36] Empowering the workforce with a voice is more than just listening to what they have to say. It is, as Guidara believes, about leveraging their unique insights and perspectives to fuel ideas, support business decisions, and inform how an organization defines and lives out its values. When leadership instead opts to disrupt or stifle agency on the individual, collective, or community level, we must ask ourselves why. Too often it is an attempt to hold onto a concentration of power among few at the top at the cost of the well-being of many. Modern leaders, on the contrary, reframe business success as the ability to make a positive impact on all their stakeholders, requiring both humility and perspective to ask for their input on how to move forward. As workers and consumers become more aware of their ability to affect change through collective action, organizations, whether they are ready or not, will be forced to listen and respond to the demands of a largely reasonable employee base. And they should; we cannot hope to make progress without the buy-in of a motivated and committed workforce.

CHAPTER

6

Well-being

"When we prioritize our well-being, everything else in our life gets better, including our products, including our performance at work, including our success."

—Arianna Huffington[1]

In 2019, the World Health Organization officially recognized burnout as a diagnosable syndrome resulting from "chronic workplace stress that has not been meaningfully managed."[2] Burnout has been studied since the 1970s, when psychologists started to observe a phenomenon among workers, especially in the health and human services industry, experiencing symptoms like exhaustion, emotional detachment, quickness to anger, headaches, and gastrointestinal issues. In the wake of 1960s idealism when many in society imagined a life not centered around work and were optimistic about the progress of society, the 1970s brought with them a disillusionment with institutions that had failed to deliver meaningful change in the war on poverty and civil rights and dragged on an unpopular and devastating war in Vietnam. Moreover, in the workplace, historians now see 1974 as a watershed moment when increases in worker productivity were no longer matched by a commensurate increase in wages – a trend that remains true to this day. Historian Rick Perlstein describes the decade as "The continuous readjustment of expectations – *downward*."[3]

Detached, cynical, and exhausted could very well describe the workforce we participate in today, over 50 years later. As a leader, providing people with a sense of purpose and agency is an important part of the architecture of a healthy organization. But the foundation of a functional, productive, and progressive company is well-being. Today, we're faced with a mental health pandemic, in many ways born from the same type of disillusionment the public faced starting in 1974 and exacerbated by the likes of social media's echo chamber and culture of comparison and perfection. Reeling from a global pandemic, geopolitical strife, economic downturn, cultural polarization, and racial unrest, our society is struggling simply to cope. Meanwhile, in our workplaces, many leaders facing pressure to perform in an unfavorable market are forgoing humanity.

As leaders, we must do what's in our control to support well-being and meet the human needs of our workforce. And while many today may not feel prepared to meet that task, they are responsible for finding a way to manage it; nearly 70% of people say that their manager has more impact on their mental health than their therapist or doctor does.[4] As a result of the context in which we live, the workplace has transformed into an embassy-like organization that provides safety, security, and opportunity in an uncertain world. With leaders as their ambassadors, companies are now responsible for doing what's in their power to support and promote the well-being of their people. The call to action is as necessary as it is urgent.

The Measurable and Immeasurable Impact of Well-being

Too often, CEOs are wary of extending benefits to include the likes of wellness stipends, comprehensive parental leave and caregiving policies, sabbatical programs, and flexible working models. These types of leaders focus only on the dollars they perceive to be flying out the door for "nice to have" perks that will negatively affect their bottom line. They view the opportunity in front of them with a mindset of scarcity and a belief that investing in people's well-being is a sunk cost. Curious leaders with an expansive mindset, on the other hand, approach the question differently. Instead of asking how much it will cost, they wonder: What can we gain from investing in our people?

When we look at the data, it's clear that healthy workers are able to contribute more while costing companies less. In fact, the average return on investment for employee wellness programs is six to one.[5] When leaders invest in well-being, they see positive returns in productivity and engagement and a decline in turnover and absenteeism, adding up to profound gains for their business overall. Johnson & Johnson, for example, estimated in 2010 that their wellness programs saved them $250 million in healthcare costs over the past decade,[6] while a third-party study in 2023 found that companies that invest in high-quality mental health care solutions for their teams save approximately $2,300 per person in health plan spend.[7] When well-being is disregarded, on the other hand, the consequences are hard to ignore: Gallup estimates that employee burnout costs businesses around the world $322 billion in lost productivity and turnover, and $20 billion in additional lost opportunity due to struggling or suffering employees.[8]

In 2023, anxiety was listed as the number-one reason for mental health leave. As ComPsych founder and CEO Richard Chaifetz explains, "From the pandemic to ongoing conflicts in Gaza and Ukraine, civil unrest, an unpredictable economy, and increasingly polarized political rhetoric surrounding elections, there is a persistent underlying feeling of apprehension and worry." Even before the pandemic, declining mental health was on the rise: from 2017 to 2023, absences related to mental health increased by 300% in the workplace. The pervasiveness of burnout, anxiety, and mental illness in our communities and our organizations is an urgent and growing problem that leaders must address today.[9]

Although these staggering statistics are overwhelming, supporting employee wellness is not always as complicated or costly as it seems. First and foremost, solving this issue comes back to our ability as leaders to center decision-making around human requirements. When we approach our challenges through this lens, reducing anxiety and increasing well-being can start with simple solutions such as increasing flexibility to allow people – especially parents and caregivers – more autonomy, or creating more humane policies around sick leave and personal time off. Expanding bereavement leave to include loved ones outside of the immediate family (even pets) and extending time off in the case of miscarriage, for example, are low-cost, high-impact ways that show employees they are valued and cared for as people, not just as workers. The gains from a workforce that feels seen, safe, and supported in their humanity are in some ways immeasurable.

Other initiatives, like investing in childcare programs for employees, may entail greater operational overhead and effort, but can provide incredible advantages to an organization that commits to supporting their people in this way. A 2024 study from Moms First and Boston Consulting Group reports that companies that invest in childcare benefits have seen up to a 425% return on investment. Considering that childcare costs increased by 32% from 2019 to 2023, many women have simply opted out of returning to the workforce after giving birth because they would operate at a loss financially. And, as we've discussed in earlier chapters, those who stay in the workforce are more susceptible to burnout, as they attempt to balance work and family. This void of social and financial support for women, who make up most caregivers in our society, is costing both businesses and our economy: Inconsistent access to childcare costs companies $13 billion in turnover annually, even though retaining just 1% of the eligible employees for childcare benefits could cover the cost completely.[10]

The well-being of an organization is inextricably linked to the well-being of its employees. From low-hanging-fruit initiatives that recognize and make space for our humanity day to day, to substantial programs with proven long-term ROI, leaders have the capacity to meaningfully change the worker experience and therefore the trajectory of their business. But formal policies and initiatives alone are not enough; it is equally important that leaders build a culture that supports and prioritizes the well-being of their people every day and that actively weeds out any attitudes, behaviors, or ways of working that threaten to erode it. It is through this consistent commitment that leaders can contribute to building a healthier workplace community and a larger culture that values and prioritizes wellness within and outside of the workplace.

What Leaders Must Do: The Four Pillars of Worker Well-Being

In 2022, Deloitte released a study on the C-suite's role in well-being. What they found is that although organizations are increasingly aware of the importance of well-being in the workplace, executives are largely underestimating how much their teams are struggling, despite reporting poor mental health themselves (see Figure 6.1).[11]

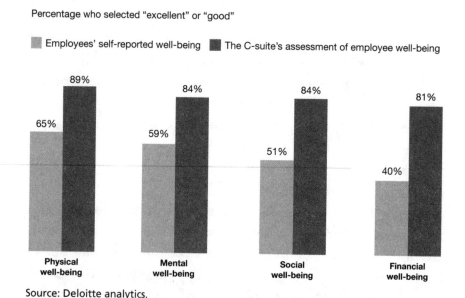

Percentage who selected "excellent" or "good"

■ Employees' self-reported well-being   ■ The C-suite's assessment of employee well-being

	Physical well-being	Mental well-being	Social well-being	Financial well-being
Employees' self-reported well-being	65%	59%	51%	40%
The C-suite's assessment	89%	84%	84%	81%

Source: Deloitte analytics.

FIGURE 6.1 The C-suite significantly underestimates how much employees are struggling with their well-being.

Of particular concern is that only 56% of employees report that they believe the executives at their company care about their well-being; meanwhile, 91% of those executives believe that their employees feel they care about them.[12] This is a startling discrepancy as we consider the impact wellness makes on a company's ability to perform. If leaders fail to recognize that their teams are struggling, how then are they to address this insidious threat to their business? Ultimately it is their responsibility to examine and confront the true conditions of their workplace and close the gap. This exercise is as strategically important as any other. Without a healthy workforce, even the best-laid business plans will fail.

The trouble is that leaders these days often don't know where to start, as the lines become blurred between public and private spheres and the world grows increasingly complex and difficult to navigate. Perhaps the paralysis many face in addressing well-being at their organization is that the topic seems too vast and therefore overwhelming, and the pressure to lead perfectly through it is too great. So let's talk briefly about what a leader's role in supporting wellness isn't, before we get into what it is. It's unreasonable to expect leaders to become an all-in-one personal coach, advisor, therapist, and business mentor. We each have our limits in terms of experience, qualification, and social boundaries. And that's okay. Nobody can be everything to everyone; the quality of our true gifts is watered down when we try. But within the sphere of influence as leaders at work, there are in fact five concrete areas where we must contribute to and safeguard wellness. The impact we have by focusing on these areas for our teams is not small; they create a powerful and positive ripple effect within the lives of the people who work with us that extends beyond the boundaries of the office.

Predictability and Flexibility

The foundation of all workplace well-being is safety – psychological and physical. As discussed in Part I, feeling safe is the distinguishing and unifying factor among high-performing teams that excel in collaboration, agility, and innovation. Leaders create safe spaces for their teams in several ways, including the vital work of fostering inclusive and equitable workplaces for marginalized groups. But more broadly, one of the most effective behaviors leaders can adopt to help people feel psychologically safe is transparent communication and clear expectation setting.

As many of you may have experienced yourselves, a root cause of workplace anxiety and burnout is uncertainty around expectations and unpredictable leadership. Leaders must create environments where "the big stuff" is as predictable as clockwork: how the team prioritizes and sets goals, how performance is measured and communicated, how work is assigned and tracked, and how their managers handle hard conversations, to name a few. Uncertainty disrupts productivity and generates a baseline anxiety that stunts the flow of work. This looks like constant interference of new "urgent" projects, a boss's erratic or disproportionate response to disappointing news, and needing to be "on call" every weekend to respond to last-minute requests. It feels like constantly waiting for the other shoe to drop.

Clear communication is especially critical around feedback. At any given moment, workers should know exactly what their manager thinks of their performance – both the areas they excel in and those that need improvement. An employee should never wonder if they're good at their job or fear without evidence that they will lose it; it's a leader's responsibility to champion and support their growth through candid and compassionate conversations around their growth and development. Feeling safe at work means that you and your manager are playing on the same team and by the same rules. You know what you can expect in most reasonable scenarios, and you trust the other to play with honesty and integrity as you work toward the same goal. It is only then that you are in fact free enough to contribute the full scope of your talent and voice to the team you're playing for.

It may seem strange to present the idea of predictability next to flexibility, but contrary to what you may think, these two concepts go hand in hand. Psychological safety born out of predictability is the springboard for allowing flexibility in the workplace; when a team operates from a place of mutual trust, there is more opportunity to successfully adapt how, when, and where we work to meet our human needs and better balance work and life. While Christie was at Deloitte, the idea of flexibility and predictability was a cornerstone of the culture based on the idea that outcome is more important than strict working hours. Teams created predictability for each other by aligning clearly on what needs to get done and by when, and then coordinated on their schedules and the coverage needed from one another to attend to personal needs. By doing so, employees were able to take time during the day to attend a yoga class, coach their kid's soccer team, or attend therapy and then return to work at a communicated time to review their project's status and continue to move it forward. Because of the level of trust and safety within the team, this did not hinder their workflow, productivity, or impact. Rather, it enhanced it.

In the post-pandemic workplace, the debate around whether employees need to be in the office to be productive and innovative has been divisive. The truth is that fully remote work is not necessarily right for every company, but it is critical for employees' engagement, creativity, and motivation that their organizations enable a degree of flexibility in how, when, and where work gets done. In other words, employers must work with the human need for agency and autonomy and not against it to achieve the desired results. Fundamentally, it means building a framework for work that enables flexibility and empowers personal choice.

Consider that while we often speak to full-time employees working nine-to-five, many workers are clocking in well over 40 hours a week and are online checking emails and messages throughout the day. Meanwhile, the school day often runs from around 8 a.m. to 3 p.m., creating a logistical nightmare for parents and putting them in the difficult position of juggling the schedules and expectations of work, family, and the extra expense of childcare during the workweek. Offering flexibility in where and when they get their work done would be a straightforward way to relieve that mental load and promote greater well-being within and outside of the office.

More disturbing is the fact that so few workplaces in the United States offer adequate paid leave for new mothers and flexibility around their return to work. The average maternity leave in the US is 10 weeks, a period that doctors consider inadequate for recovering from childbirth and adjusting to the arrival of a new baby. An OBGYN explains, "As each trimester of pregnancy brought changes for the woman and baby, the period after delivery is a continuation of change. Inadequate maternity leave can lead not only to anxiety and depression, but also relationship issues and the inability to return to work."[13] Ultimately, it should be a woman's choice to decide when and how she transitions back to work after giving birth. And in the absence of a federally mandated minimum leave for new mothers, it is a company's responsibility to ensure that women have adequate and flexible options that support a smooth transition back into the workforce. Empowering women with this autonomy is among the most humane practices an organization can champion in support of mental and physical well-being.

On the most basic level, flexibility is about letting people be people. It makes time and space for them to attend doctors' appointments, work with their own productivity rhythms, take a long lunch to meet a visiting friend, or have a break in the afternoon for a walk or a power nap. These very human activities do not hurt their productivity – they enable it. Research from the Upwork Research Institute found that companies that excel in flexible work are nearly twice as likely to describe their organization as agile compared to those that do not use such practices. In addition, leaders from companies with flexible work models are more confident about their organization's future, with 55% expressing complete confidence compared to only 27% of their peers.[14] This benefit stems not only from an increased sense of autonomy within the workforce, but also from the reduction of burnout.[15] Of course, radical flexibility is balanced by governance; employers provide the options for and the rules by which flexibility is possible. Within these boundaries, workers can simultaneously exercise their agency, tend to their well-being, and meet the clearly communicated expectations of their management.

Mental Health Resources

Half of the world's population will develop a mental health disorder in their lifetime.[16] Let that statistic sink in as you think about the humans you interact with daily in your personal and professional life. As more data and research emerges on the impact on our well-being of social media, the pandemic, increased isolation, and collective trauma, one thing becomes clear: declining mental health is a global emergency. It is a silent and life-threatening pandemic that will ultimately wreak as much or more havoc on our society and its workforce as COVID-19.

In the workplace we see that the poor state of mental health negatively affects engagement, motivation, creativity, and collaboration. On average, people suffering from depression miss 31.4 days of work each year, while chronic stress and anxiety prevent those at work from participating fully. These symptoms of mental illness result in a 35% reduction in productivity and a loss of $2,10.5 billion to the US economy each year in the form of absenteeism, lowered productivity, and medical costs. People who are not struggling with their mental health spend 23% less effort on creative tasks comparatively. Researchers from Qualtrics who conducted studies on the relationship between mental health and work productivity explain that "positive mental health is associated with a faster, slicker runway toward creativity and innovation – and health in general."[17]

Most leaders, of course, are not equipped to monitor and manage the mental health of their teams alone. But there are a variety of resources available today to help support organizations and their management to provide resources for workers suffering from mental health issues, or those looking to actively build healthy preventative habits around their well-being. Yet unfortunately, many workers report that accessing mental health resources is a challenge for them due to poor insurance coverage, difficulty determining covered services, trouble finding providers, uncertainty around which resources are available, and long wait times to get an appointment.[18] Providing comprehensive healthcare packages that include mental health services – and communicating about these options clearly – is important. But these days, employers are also able to supplement this fundamental benefit with a slew of tech solutions that meet the various health needs of their people. Some even leverage AI to detect signs of mental health distress and confidentially provide resources to those in need.[19]

Platforms like the on-demand virtual therapy app BetterHelp, or enterprise coaching solutions like BetterUp, are two examples of resources companies can invest in to promote ongoing care to their teams. Moreover, providing access to or subsidizing activities proven to combat stress and improve mood, like exercise and meditation, can contribute to building healthy habits within the workforce that ultimately benefit productivity and innovation. With so many incredible resources at our disposal and so much to be gained from implementing them, there are few reasons that would justify an employer opting out of offering these services.

Modeling Well-being

None of the previous pillars can be as effective without leaders taking an active role in modeling well-being for their teams. The legacy of command-and-control leadership that made little to no space for feelings has left its mark, as have centuries of stigmatization around mental illness. There are countless members of our workforce who fear setting a boundary or showing any vulnerability at the risk of being judged, punished, or dismissed. Leaders play a critical role in destigmatizing mental illness and creating cultures that demonstrably prioritize mental health care.

In the simplest terms, leaders must lead. They cannot promote practices within their teams such as logging off on time and only responding to emails during working hours if they themselves are setting a different standard by example. They cannot talk about the importance of taking PTO if year after year they fail to use all of their vacation days. They cannot warn employees of burnout if they don't block space in their own calendars to care for themselves or stay home sick when they are in fact sick. In advocating for the well-being of the workforce, leaders must also prove with their behaviors and actions that it is safe and accepted to care for oneself. In cultures where those who are perceived to "tough it out" or "burn the midnight oil" are valorized, this form of leadership is a radical act.

Meanwhile in countries like France and states like California, we've seen legislation introduced that outlaws employers from contacting their employees after working hours. So pervasive has the habit of work encroaching on people's personal lives become, and so dire is the state of mental health, that the government must intervene to legalize the "right to disconnect" – rightly so, and yet a sad reflection on the state of leadership that we have failed to safeguard people's right to a private life ourselves first. It begs the question: In pursuit of relentless productivity, have we lost the plot on what it's all for? We've certainly missed the mark in terms of recognizing the crucial relationship between human well-being, true innovation, and meaningful progress.

For leaders, it is not only that modeling wellness practices is good for their teams. It is also good for them. (Yes, it's true: leaders are people, too.) We all require rest, reflection, and care to be fully present and engaged in our jobs and with our colleagues. It is not a luxury but a responsibility of leadership to prioritize our own mental health. The more grace we give to ourselves, the more we can offer those we lead.

Relationship Building

One of the most powerfully simple tools that a leader can use in the support of a healthier organization is the time they spend with their team members. In his book *Love and Work: How to Find What You Love, Love What You Do, and Do It for the Rest of Your Life*, Marcus Buckingham urges leaders to think about building loving relationships at work. Of course, he does not mean that relationships with our colleagues ought to mimic those in our personal lives in terms of their level of intimacy; rather, his point is that in a loving relationship, the aim is to truly see and understand the other and support their journey toward becoming their fullest, truest self. This, he argues, is at the heart of leadership, requiring managers to give enough of their time and attention to their teams to truly know and see them. Here, the details are important: what makes each person tick, what drags them down, and what on the horizon excites them. Leaders and their direct reports need not be friends; but a leader must extend their boundaries to know their people well enough that they can tap into and leverage their unique sense of purpose and their talents in a way that ultimately benefits the individual and business.

In this way, curiosity is a powerful tool for leaders to uncover the true motivations and the perhaps yet-to-be-discovered potential of their workforce – the unlock that leads to more satisfaction and greater contribution overall. It is also the key to leading with compassion. By building relationships with team members, leaders gain insights into their moods, habits, and patterns, making it easier to recognize when something may be off, and in turn easier to extend help. By leading with kindness, respect, and care, they build greater trust within their team that they are a judgment-free zone and a resource at their disposal for when they are struggling. Gone are the days of transactional leadership; what is required of leaders today is an investment and commitment to supporting their people's full humanity.

CHAPTER

7

Connection

"My humanity is bound up in yours, for we can only be human together."

—Desmond Tutu[1]

When it comes to the evolution of an increasingly lonely and isolated society, psychotherapist Esther Perel warns of "the other AI": artificial intimacy.[2] Paradoxically, technology has the power both to connect people and to erode the quality of our social relationships. While social media and other digital platforms help people to find common ground, stay in touch from afar, and bond over shared interests, our devices also distract us from the people right in front of us. As a result, the quality of our relationships is suffering, and even when we are in rooms full of people, many of us feel lonelier than ever. And yet connection is vital to our well-being and key to human thriving, which means that it is essential to business.

At work, where most communication, even in the office, happens over digital channels, creating genuine connection has grown to be a challenging endeavor. In a study by Airspeed conducted after the pandemic, executives cited it as the number-one challenge they face in their organizations.[3] Many point their fingers at remote work for this predicament, but it is not in fact a specific working model that puts human connection at risk. Within in-office environments, we also see relationship building transforming into a lost art, with workers spending hours coordinating over email and messaging programs like Slack and Microsoft Teams, and many lamenting unnecessary, unproductive, and unfocused meetings. Defining our failure to connect by the increase of technology and distributed work alone is shortsighted and incomplete. As we have seen, there is a clear case for how technology and flexibility empower and enable greater productivity and quality overall. The question of declining connection is not entirely about where we spend time with our teams, how often we communicate, or the structure of work – it is most profoundly about the quality of time spent together, which depends on our capacity as leaders to be fully present and extend our boundaries in service of our teams.

Developments in asynchronous and distributed work have in many ways improved the way we live. And while we have made much progress in increasing flexibility and leveraging technology to our advantage in recent years, leaders have failed to evolve how they build connections within their teams to keep pace with this new landscape. As we emerged from the COVID-19 lockdown, there was a lot of enthusiasm about the widespread adoption of new working models, but we also faced an increasingly isolated society with weakened social skills and a deep longing for restored connection. After decades of following social norms developed within the four walls of an office, the pandemic abruptly forced people into a new way of working without a companion guide for the new rules of social interaction. In response to complaints about declining corporate culture and failed collaboration, leaders filled their teams' days with more meetings, more virtual or in-person social events, and more Slack channels to patch the hole – only to find themselves facing the same feedback. What was missing?

In Priya Parker's book *The Art of Gathering*, she introduces the idea that bringing people together can only be successful when we understand the "why" behind it. Only then can we successfully decide on the "how": what form it takes, who needs to be there, the role they play, and what to communicate so that people can show up prepared and in the right mindset (essential to creating psychological safety). By planning our gatherings with this level of purpose, transparency, and care, she argues that we generate "the possibility of creating something memorable, even transformative" for the people participating.[4] So often when addressing the disconnection in our workforce, we skip forward to the "what," reacting with quick solutions to bring people together but failing to address the root of the problem by finding a meaningful "why" to gather people around. This only results in further disconnection. Developing a deeper sense of trust, belonging, and bonding with our people requires greater intentionality with how we create connection points and model being present.

Of course, the importance of connection is not lost on leaders; 96% of executives in the US believe that workers who feel connected with each other are more motivated and productive. Meanwhile, workers cite that feeling disconnected from their colleagues is a top reason they would quit a job.[5] Feeling connected at work is about the human need to be seen, heard, and valued – to know that we matter. Connection underpins our ability to unite around a shared purpose, be empowered to exercise our agency, and feel secure enough to prioritize our own well-being. Relationship building is the gateway to meeting the other human needs that motivate us to contribute fully at work and form a company culture that begets loyalty and enthusiasm for the work at hand. Connection not only makes work more enjoyable but is the spark by which we achieve greater innovation because it creates the psychological safety that's needed to collaborate and introduce new and radical ideas.

Safeguarding Connection in the Age of AI and Distributed Work

It's still true that as technology becomes central to the way we work, it is essential that we safeguard the social skills that have been and always will be critical to our collective well-being. AI and technology have already replaced many human-to-human connection points with human-to-machine interactions, from customer service chatbots and self-checkout to the fact that we now direct our questions to Google and ChatGPT instead of our local library. The fact is that as social interactions become fewer and farther between and the quality of our face-to-face interactions diminishes, the health of our society suffers. As Kate Murphy illustrates in her article for the *New York Times*, "We're All Socially Awkward Now," "Research on prisoners, hermits, soldiers, astronauts, polar explorers and others who have spent extended periods in isolation indicates social skills are like muscles that atrophy from lack of use. People separated from society – by circumstance or by choice – report feeling more socially anxious, impulsive, awkward and intolerant when they return to normal life."[6]

You may be thinking at this point that we are unraveling our own argument for workforce flexibility; that the answer once again comes back to a return to the office as the essential hub for community building. But we are here to reiterate that the answer to the erosion of our social fabric as a society is not found in a one-size-fits-all working model. We know that people need flexibility in order to manage their complex lives and schedules with more ease and greater contentment, and that they require agency in defining how, when, and if they work.

We also know that these factors benefit a more inclusive and equitable workplace, and that flexibility allows more people to participate in the workforce. To ignore these truths that ultimately benefit productivity and innovation within our organizations by arbitrarily forcing people back into an office is a failure of leadership and creativity. When we force employees back into the office without good cause, what we are actually communicating is that we do not trust them to do the work that they are required to do. The result is almost always the further erosion of our workplace cultures. In showing our people that we do not trust them, we give them reason to not trust us. A greater sense of community within our teams is not dependent on a specific working model but on how leaders connect people through a shared purpose and the support of their humanity. In other words, how we engage our workforce and connect with them matters much more than where we do it.

Multiple things can of course be true. We know that people are lonelier and more isolated than ever, that technology is not always helping, and that a forced return to office is not the panacea for increasing connection across our teams. When we say that it is a failure of leadership and creativity when CEOs force people whose work is not location-dependent back into an office, our meaning is twofold. First, by attempting to solve their business problems by increasing control and tightening their grip on an already largely disengaged and burnt-out workforce, these leaders demonstrate that they are out of touch and unwilling to take accountability for the real reasons their performance is suffering. And second, they are failing to think innovatively about how the very technology and working models they cite as hindering connection and creativity in their workforce can also be leveraged in their service. The latter argument, however, is entirely dependent on a new leadership mindset that approaches culture building with a greater sense of purpose and intention and a nuanced evaluation of where and how technology and flexibility work in service of your people and where they work against it.

Once again, leaders must ask this question: What do the humans within my organization require to thrive? This question has several follow-ups to consider within this context, including:

- What must I do as a leader to forge a greater sense of connection between my people and our company's purpose?

- Which tools and working models support my workforce's efficiency and effectiveness, thereby creating greater space for human-to-human collaboration and connection?

- How can I create stronger personal bonds between the individuals on my team and within my own relationships with each of them?

The Building Blocks of a Connected Organization

The good news is that the opportunity to create connection as a leader exists and can be carried through on several levels within an organization and its ecosystem. First, on the macro level, alignment on an organization's purpose and values provides a foundation around which employees can rally and find common ground. It is a leader's job to unite their teams around this shared mission and call back to it as often as possible in their daily work as a reminder of what their people's efforts and teamwork is all for. It is the glue by which team members will be able to first relate to each other when joining an organization, and what they will harken back to when they are challenged by disagreement and disappointment. It is also what they will come together to celebrate when they reach an important milestone or hit a project out of the park. Understanding what your company's purpose and values mean to your employees will allow you to better leverage their passion and enthusiasm toward that shared mission, which will, by default, bring people closer.

Within departments and smaller teams, creating connection may seem easier, or at least less daunting. Yet leaders today often struggle with engaging their teams and incentivizing their full participation in brainstorms, meetings, and feedback sessions. Group dynamics are by nature challenging, and leaders know all too well how the energy in a room can be positively or negatively affected by the attitude just one person brings to the table. As we think about what it means to create connection within the workplace, we must also think about the smaller subcultures within our companies and how to support healthy dynamics within those ecosystems. Too often in group settings, we fail to recognize how a sense of connection and shared purpose among peers helps us to reach our objectives more effectively within a meeting. We spend more time thinking about what we want out of people instead of what people need to engage: to understand their role, how to contribute, and, essentially, that they are safe to be themselves – to be human.

According to a survey conducted by Atlassian, 72% of meetings are reported to be ineffective, with 70% of those surveyed reporting that these meetings fail to create connection with their colleagues.[7] These failed gatherings are not only frustrating and hard on morale, but they also waste people's time, negatively impact their focus, hinder true collaboration, and ultimately erode an organization's productivity. What bonds us as teams and leads to greater outcomes from our meetings and our performance at large is shared understanding – not only about the purpose of why we are meeting and how (the required preparation, structure, and rules of engagement), but equally important, of each other. When gathering a team together and deciding how to run a meeting, a leader must account for humanity first. In other words, what do I need to do to make people feel seen, heard, and valued on the way to our desired outcome? How do I make space for the unknown variables – how people are feeling, their energy levels, and their concerns?

The most effective meetings are run by leaders who first take time to acknowledge and get curious about the people who are joining them in the room. They take a pulse check on morale, they address any worries and concerns up front, and they are flexible in their mindset about how they can best achieve their goals based on the feedback they receive. In other words, their curiosity enables flexibility and in turn builds trust and connection with a team that knows that their humanity is not only welcome, it comes first. What this looks like in practice is nothing revolutionary, but it is profound. It is putting time in the agenda to do a show of hands in the group of how they are feeling from one to five (struggling to thriving); it's building in a 20-minute weekly feedback session to talk about what went well and what did not in the last few days; it's encouraging healthy debate and conflict by modeling it yourself and ensuring that every person in the room has a chance to share their viewpoint and expertise (especially the quieter ones).

It is equally important that we support connection between our team members by encouraging and empowering opportunities for collaboration and investing in peer-to-peer team building. By establishing a foundation of trust and belonging within the larger group, leaders make it possible for the individuals on their team to open up and rely on one another more, thereby forming their own relationships that can exist independent of leadership. To the benefit of their work, employees who feel connected to one another will turn to each other more often for help and to pull in complementary expertise. And, together with feeling valued by their leader for their own unique voice and contribution, they will celebrate rather than compete with each other's successes.

Of course, one-on-ones are also critical opportunities to build connection with our team members, but to an even greater depth. Here, a leader's objective is to create space to get to know individuals better and provide them the support they need to succeed in their roles. These relationships are of course different from the personal relationships we share in our private lives, but they should be handled with the same care, compassion, and interest, albeit in a different context. The time spent with people on our team should be focused on better understanding their drivers, motivations, and interests – and, on the contrary, what drains, discourages, and drags them down. In one-on-one relationships, a leader's job is to uncover how their team members can best contribute to the organization based on the intersection of this information, which in turn allows us to position people in roles, projects, and learning opportunities they enjoy and feel valued in, ultimately empowering them to thrive.

In a practical sense, spending time with people on our team is also about managing their workload to prevent burnout, creating a safe space for sharing new ideas and out-of-the-box thinking, and collaborating with them on their growth and development. Successfully navigating these topics with team members requires leaders to make themselves available and accessible to people and to be fully present for their conversations. It also depends greatly on a leader's ability to put aside their own interests to serve the person in front of them with curiosity, honesty, and kindness. In return, employees who feel seen, heard, and safe offer back to an organization their commitment and full engagement.

Investing in Leadership Skills that Build Connection

Research has shown without equivocation that "quality social support, social integration, and regular communication among co-workers of all levels are key in preventing chronic work stress and workplace burnout."[8] In the face of global socioeconomic change, technological disruption, and an epidemic of loneliness, building connection as a leader has the power to increase a workforce's resilience and positively impact their mental health, as we have discussed in the previous chapter. It should go without saying that these benefits to people ultimately benefit business. In fact, according to the US Surgeon General's findings, workplace connectedness has the ability to improve creativity and work quality, and may even "influence career advancements, income, and overall economic stability."[9] What we stand to gain as employers from investing in our relationships at work is great. What society stands to gain from a more connected community is greater. To meet the needs of a workplace that not only yearns for but requires connection to excel, leaders will be required to further develop and invest in the skills that support building connection with their team members and across their organization. The first requirement in doing so is that they embrace their own humanity, and thereby role-model that it is in fact a leadership quality and an asset to prioritize it.

PART

What Leaders Must Do

CHAPTER

8

Soft Skills Are Power Skills

"Technology alone is not enough. It's technology married with the liberal arts, married with the humanities, that yields the results that makes our hearts sing."[1]

—Steve Jobs

In a 2011 article for *Harvard Business Review*, Horace Dediu examines what he considers the greatest lesson from Steve Jobs for companies today. He writes, "We should look forward to the post-Jobs era as that time when large companies gained the ability to intertwine multiple core competencies. A time when humanism balanced corporatism. A time when we came to reconcile the rational and spiritual."[2] Jobs, and Dediu in turn, had an almost prescient understanding of the realities of the modern workplace and the need for a more humanist approach to business. During the Renaissance, as we spoke about in the introduction of this book, humanism rejected the more medieval scholarly philosophies and stoicism of the preceding age and championed the importance of human interests and values. In our modern era, technological advancement has given way to a similar cultural movement, one that reminds us again to center humanity in our march toward progress.

While it's clear that we're in the midst of a great cultural change, fueled by various technological, socioeconomic, and geopolitical factors, far too many organizations today are operating with humanist principles far in the background. As a result, we've seen phenomena unfold like quiet quitting, the Great Resignation, and women leaving the workforce in record numbers. In an ever-tightening labor market, leaders are struggling to find people with the necessary skills, talent, and capabilities to compete on the global stage and move their business forward. Still, while CEOs lament their greatest vulnerabilities as finding talent, keeping talent, and managing talent in a distributed workforce, few have evaluated their leadership principles or taken risks to overhaul how they manage their teams. In doing so, the essentials required to meet the modern workforce are overlooked.

Solving this very real humanity-at-work crisis will take more than leaders learning how to leverage new technologies; it requires the expansion and prioritization of the "softer side" of leadership, including the further development of management capabilities far too often ignored but urgently needed to meaningfully engage the workforce. The crisis at hand is a human problem first, and to win in today's talent markets, leaders must capture the hearts and minds of their teams by establishing profound trust and practicing vulnerability, and ultimately by suspending self-interest. *If left unaddressed, the failure of leadership to evolve with a human-first lens will continue to cost businesses – and society at large – billions of dollars in productivity as workers disengage, quit, and fail to reenter the workforce.* Ultimately, technology alone will not be able to keep pace and effectively meet the very *human* needs of today's workforce.

Robert Solow once famously quipped, "You can see the computer age everywhere but in the productivity statistics."[3] Technology can only take us so far without the adoption of a new kind of leadership, and soft skills will be the differentiator for organizations in the war for skills and the creation of greater business value. As we take a closer look at our new leadership imperative, we must understand the underlying forces demanding this essential leadership change and what's at stake for those unwilling or unable to engage in the very hard discipline of soft skills.

When AI Masters Hard Skills Better Than Most Leaders

With the increased adoption of new technology in the workplace, the hard skills we once delegated exclusively to leadership roles are increasingly in competition with what artificial intelligence excels at. Previously in the book we discussed the danger zone of gray-collar skills that are quickly becoming automated by technology advancements. Historically, the skills and jobs that usually require a college education have been deemed safe from technology due to their professional nature, but this is no longer so. As you thought about the gray-collar category of workers at risk of being outpaced and overlooked in your own organization, did leadership ever come to mind? What's fascinating to consider is that according to the research of 500 CEOs, 49% believed that artificial intelligence should automate or replace most of their jobs. This compares to only 20% of the workforce who felt the same about their own jobs.[4] The CEOs cited within the research acknowledged that a lot of their job was focused on the hard skills of running a business, and with machine learning and generative AI on the rise, many felt that these technologies could likely do these tasks at least as well, if not better.

A striking statistic reveals that more than one-third (34%) of knowledge workers perceive these technologies not merely as tools for efficiency but as a substitute for effective leadership.[5] This perception underscores a critical misunderstanding in the corporate world: Technology, no matter how advanced, cannot replace the human elements of leadership – vision, empathy, and the ability to inspire and motivate. Somehow, we've overlooked these essential human capabilities and favored a more technical leader.

But leadership is fundamentally about connecting with people, understanding their needs, and guiding them toward a common goal. Effective leaders leverage technology to enhance these connections, not to replace them. They understand that technology is a means to facilitate communication, streamline workflows, and foster collaboration. However, the core of leadership lies in the ability to drive accountability, clarity, and engagement within a team.

Accountability and clarity in roles and responsibilities are not merely administrative details; they are the bedrock of a high-performing team. Technology can aid in making these aspects more transparent and accessible, but it is the leader's responsibility to ensure that everyone in the team understands their role, feels responsible for their contributions, and is aligned with the team's objectives.

Moreover, engaging a workforce goes beyond providing them with the latest tools. It involves creating an environment where employees feel valued, understood, and motivated. Leaders must use technology to create spaces for meaningful engagement, where employees can share ideas, feedback, and collaborate in ways that enrich their work experience and personal growth.

In effect, while technologies offer numerous benefits, they serve as amplifiers of leadership qualities, not replacements. The true challenge for leaders in the digital age is to harness these tools to enhance their leadership capabilities, ensuring that technology strengthens, rather than undermines, the human connections that are the essence of effective leadership.

Furthermore, a sentiment shift is happening in real time across the workforce as they begin to work alongside advanced technologies in the workplace. In fact, one in five workers today believe that AI is better at recognizing human behavior and would trust the technology more than a human leader to understand them at work.[6] That's a shocking statistic and humbling to consider the state of leadership in many organizations today. This is especially true with the younger generation, with 47% of Gen Z workers who believe that large-language-models, like Chat GPT, are giving them better professional development and career advice than their boss.[7] As a result, they're turning more and more to AI for coaching, development, and support in place of their leaders. However, these are the very human intelligence-based soft skills that leaders are uniquely positioned to provide.

Dov Seidman, who runs a moral institute for leadership called the HOW Institute for Society, explained, "Today's leaders are facing unfamiliar challenges and ever-increasing expectations from stakeholders across society. ... They look to leaders for hope – and hope can only be fostered by leaders who bring out the best in people, who inspire collaboration, a common purpose, and future possibilities."[8] The problem according to their research is that only 10% of global leaders fall within a top tier of moral leadership behaviors. It may not be an overstatement to say that leadership is in a state of crisis. With a skills shortage looming and trust declining, it is essential that leaders embark on a new way to leverage uniquely human skills to stay ahead.

Soft Skills Are Now a Leader's Power Skills

The abuse of power and the neglect of soft skills in leadership can have devastating consequences. It may be no surprise then that in 2022, the education technology company Udemy generated multiple headlines when they recognized and reframed soft skills as power skills for today's organizations. As organizational structures flatten and formal leadership authority based on role is no longer effective for influencing, soft skills such as creativity, teamwork, empathy, critical thinking, and communication become the currency for power within an organization today. Rather than managing through formal power, which typically results in noncompliance and disengagement, today's workforce beckons a new type of leadership power – one that is leveraged by building social capital, displaying deep care, and inspiring others toward greatness.

Udemy's power skills trend analysis discovered that because of today's shifting work models, such as distributed work, flattened organizational structures, and the rise of the alternative workforce, soft skills must be referred to in a more substantive way. As discovered, a lack of measurement has pushed soft skill development to the background, rather than making it one of the most essential skills sets to be nurtured.

As an online education company, Udemy's dataset offers insight into which skills are growing in demand. And so, while many organizations may be neglecting soft skills, individuals are now focused on them as a key variable in which they choose to work for a company. Udemy reports "triple-digit growth in categories like office productivity, leadership and management, and personal growth over the past year."[9] The report also highlights skyrocketing skills in diversity and inclusion, strategic thinking, and listening, with growth rates of over 500% in five years. What's caused the spike in soft skills – or power skills, as they've been aptly renamed? We've identified two key trends that make power skills more invaluable than ever, thus requiring a change in our collective mindset and attitudes toward the impact that these human-powered capabilities have on the success of our businesses.

The Rise of the Flexible Workforce

The realities of how and where work gets done in recent years has presented new challenges for leaders. While the formal power structure may never have been ideal for the workforce, it was a rather easy way to get work done when people were together working in the same office. Power was clearly on display depending on what floor people worked on, whether they had a corner office or cubicle, and even how groups often gathered in lunchrooms based on level within the organization. While certainly not always fair or inspiring, it was a clear way to visibly organize power within a company.

As remote and hybrid models become commonplace alongside traditional in-office setups, leaders are forced to rethink how to engage their employees, including connecting with a distributed workforce, creating culture, and measuring workforce performance and engagement. Power was distributed in these remote environments almost overnight due to the pandemic as everyone appeared in the same size box on the video screen. There were no longer visible markers of power available. As the power distance increased, it became a lot less clear who was in charge. In some cases, workers remarked how much more accessible leaders became, and others lamented about the micromanaging now occurring through a remote environment. The ability for leaders to engage in soft skills, or lack thereof, became exceedingly clear during this transition to distributed work.

If these soft skills were lacking in leaders' management capabilities pre-pandemic, they are even more strained now. Employees are no longer just looking at compensation or office perks as the deciding factor to join a company, but are making decisions based on values, autonomy, agency, work environment, structure, a sense of purpose, and real evidence of diversity and inclusion efforts. Furthermore, the role of employee engagement is paramount to a company's fulfillment and commitment to stakeholder and customer value, making it crucial for leaders and their organizations to invest in the development of the power skills that contribute to a highly engaged workforce.

Research from Paychex suggests that only half of workers intend to stay with their current companies for the next 12 months.[10] Key reasons for staying include job stability and meaningful work, with flexible work hours and mental health benefits being highly valued across different generations. The research suggests that employers should enhance retention by fostering flexibility, understanding diverse benefits preferences, investing in skill development, and conducting stay interviews. It also highlights the importance of aligning job roles with employees' personal values and interests to ensure long-term commitment. (A stay interview is a meeting used to understand what parts of an employee's job keeps them coming back every day.)

There's No Hiding in the Digital Age

The rise of the internet and social media has been a powerful tool to expose companies and leaders within them who act in direct conflict to the companies' stated values or cultural norms. This is especially true in areas easily measured like inclusion, diversity, equity, and belonging. The fact is that most companies around the world have made statements about these values, and yet their executive ranks remain largely homogeneous and with little diversity at the top. In fact, in 2023 only 2% of Fortune 500 companies had a Black CEO, and only 36% of directors in this category self-identify as an underrepresented minority, even though data shows that companies in the top quartile for ethnic and cultural diversity outperformed their peers by 36% in profitability.[11]

After more than 50 years of effort, these facts are a clear failure of leadership, one that stakeholders have a declining tolerance for as the world at large becomes more educated and aware of racial, gender, and economic disparities and inequity. The increased transparency of supply chains and a consumer base connected through social media have conspired not only to give these stakeholders a voice, but the power to shape business strategy. In this dramatic reversal of economic leverage, if the relationship with stakeholders is not quickly redefined to reflect their growing power, businesses will see employees, customers, and suppliers abandon them and use social media to air their discontents to the detriment of their brand.

On the customer side we've seen the power of collective voices coming together to engage leadership at organizations to take a stand or change their operations to do less harm. For example, in the UK, McDonald's customers were growing increasingly frustrated by leadership's lack of responsiveness to cutting down on plastic consumption. McDonald's in the UK was using 1.8 million plastic straws a day, so this change would require a massive logistics and operations shift. However, it was becoming increasingly hard to ignore the nearly half a million online signatures customers generated with their own grassroots digital campaign that pronounced, "McDonald's is polluting our oceans." After this campaign began going viral, McDonald's took swift action and began developing paper straws in direct response.[12]

And digital platforms haven't given a voice just to a company's customers, but also to their workforce. We've seen this with the rise of workforce platforms like Fishbowl, Cafe Pharma, and Glassdoor that give employees a voice in how the inner working of their organizations is really going. Leadership styles and culture are often the most discussed topics within these forums, with workers calling out, very publicly, poor leadership behavior at their companies. Research has found and directly correlated employees' views voiced on these platforms to the satisfaction of customers. In fact, Glassdoor has found that each 1-star improvement in an employer's company rating by an employee is associated with a 1.3-point increase in customer satisfaction.[13] The customer and employee opinions are connected more strongly than before as they raise their voices and ultimately awareness throughout digital platforms that result in profound transparency.

The other concern for leaders today in a remote digital environment is the use of video recordings that tend to go viral as employees post videos of how their leaders manage or even fire them. In 2024, there was much media attention given as younger workers began posting TikToks of how their managers let them go. In wake of numerous layoffs in the technology industry, and with workers fed up on how these were being handled, they took to social media to transparently share their experience in real time. Legal and ethical considerations aside for these recordings, the reality is they generated brand damage for leaders at companies who lacked the soft skills when making hard decisions.

Three Cautionary Tales

Christie once advised the chief people officer of a company she was working with by saying "our insides have to match our outsides." What Christie meant was that the rhetoric about their company values and purpose in marketing materials and talking points had to be an honest reflection of their internal behavior and decision-making as leaders. Many leaders have learned the hard way, and very publicly, that when their brand messaging is hollow, engaged and empowered consumer and employee stakeholders are quick to find out – and call it out. Consider the following examples and heed their lessons to chart a different course.

For a long time, technology companies have been the darling of the business world because of their unprecedented valuations, transforming industries almost overnight. Uber was recognized as a disruptive company, founded in 2009 and valued at over $71 billion in less than a decade. But their relentless pursuit of the bottom line cost them and their founder, Travis Kalanick, their reputation. It was a direct failure of leadership.

An investigation found that Mr. Kalanick created a systematic culture of discrimination and sexual harassment. Furthermore, Uber drivers claimed to be victims of psychological manipulation, as the company pursued profits at the expense of their drivers.[14] Public videos soon flooded the internet showing how Kalanick interacted with his drivers and workforce. As Uber started to lose profits, the CEO eventually admitted the problem wasn't with the business, but with leadership. He wrote to his staff referencing a video that went viral, "It's clear this video is a reflection of me – and the criticism we've received is a stark reminder that I must fundamentally change as a leader and grow up. This is the first time I've been willing to admit that I need leadership help and I intend to get it."[15] However, pressure from investors referencing his failure of leadership became too great, and he was ultimately required to step down in 2017. Since his departure, Uber has begun the long journey of repairing their internal culture and external reputation to regain financial footing. Since Travis's departure, the company became profitable for the very first time and achieved record stock performance in early 2024.

Another example of a failure of leadership comes from the former CEO and co-founder of Papa John's Pizza, John Schnatter. An organization externally known for its quality pizza ingredients was internally known for its "bro culture," which tolerated sexual harassment, violating employee privacy, and favoritism.[16] When Papa John's, a top NFL sponsor and advertiser, began to struggle financially, the CEO blamed it on the political environment of the NFL, citing the league's "poor leadership" in response to demonstrations during the national anthem.[17] His public statement was perceived as supporting racism, as many NFL players at the time were choosing not to stand for the national anthem in silent protest of police brutality and racial injustice. Sales plummeted even further after these remarks were made, and John Schnatter was almost immediately asked to step down from his CEO position due to the public's response.

In fact, Papa John's corporate revenue fell 5% in the first quarter versus the prior year, with net income down 40% partly because of the blunder. To make matters worse, John Schnatter, no longer operating as CEO but serving on the company's board, made direct racist comments while on a call with the brand's marketing agency. The marketing agency immediately canceled their contract with Papa John's, and Mr. Schnatter was formally removed from his board position as well. Following this next crisis, Papa John's began the slow process of culture change, emphasizing and investing in diversity, equity, and inclusion programs.[18] An HR executive at the company said of their efforts, "As this work continues, the company's [Papa John's] continuing culture transformation will include a heightened focus on the voice of the employee. Previously, leadership looked primarily at representative data to inform DE&I strategy; now, that focus is expanding to qualitative as well, such as through the Pizza Pulse surveys, which solicit anonymous feedback on everything from their wellness to the culture of inclusion." Indeed, the only way forward for Papa John's was to double down – not on business acumen but on the soft skills required to lead today's workforce. These are just a couple of examples among many others that have suffered similar reputational and brand impact directly because of leadership behaviors.

But the issue of leadership ignoring the soft side extends far beyond the United States. In 2021, Gorillas, a German grocery delivery startup that rapidly achieved unicorn status, faced significant worker unrest. Employees, earning €10.50 per hour under 12-month contracts, protested against low pay, late payments, understaffing, and inadequate safety measures. Their collective action, sparked by the sudden firing of a colleague, led to wildcat strikes and protests, exposing deep-rooted issues within the fast-growing company. Despite the workers' protests, the company responded by firing several dozen employees who participated in the strikes, underlining the tension between rapid business growth and workers' rights.[19] The company later laid off hundreds of employees in 2022 and was acquired shortly after, unable to stand apart from a crowded market.[20]

As we've discovered, not leaning into the soft side of leadership can have grave consequences for leaders and be disastrous to an organization's bottom line. And while many argue that leaders without soft skills have always existed and done so successfully, the emergence of a more empowered workforce and a hyper-digital environment has made it much more difficult for their mishaps to go unnoticed. These developments require a new set of skills from leaders, beyond the traditional role of planning, organizing, and directing resources. Leaders must evolve and expand their capabilities, considering ethical and moral considerations in pace with the world around them.

The New Power Skills

In today's leadership lexicon, "soft skills" must be rebranded as "power skills" – a testament to their newfound recognition as the cornerstone of effective leadership. Power skills encapsulate the critical, nontechnical abilities that allow leaders to engage, influence, and mobilize their teams with empathy and vision. They are the backbone of leadership, defined not by titles, authority, or tenure, but by the capacity to resonate with and uplift others around them.

These skills embody the art of communication, the grace of empathy, and the foresight of strategic thinking, enabling leaders not just to direct, but to inspire. They transform leaders into catalysts for change, visionaries who can articulate a compelling future that others eagerly want to help realize. Such leaders don't command action through authority; they inspire action through a shared sense of purpose and a deep connection to the collective mission.

The repeated findings of organizational behaviorists and industrial-organizational psychologists underscore this truth: People exceed expectations not because of an obligation to formal power structures, but because they feel a profound connection to their work's purpose and the community around them. Leaders vested with formal authority have a unique opportunity to harness this insight. By embracing power skills, they can lead in a way that attracts and inspires, paving the way for innovations and achievements that were once beyond imagination. But doing so requires a new frame leaders have around their power.

How to Softly Leverage Power

An increasingly informed workforce has spurred a need for leaders to increase efforts in building trust and transparency in the workplace. In 2021, the former CEO of Campbell's, Denise Morrison, told *Forbes*, "The single most important ingredient in the recipe for success is transparency because transparency builds trust."[21] Similarly, Microsoft CEO Satya Nadella has talked at length about how soft skills are in fact the new hard skills for leaders: "I don't think empathy is a soft skill. In fact, it's the hardest skill we learn – to relate to the world, to relate to people that matter the most to us."[22]

Prioritizing people requires a new understanding of what being a leader means. We must make a hard pivot to embrace and develop the power skills that ultimately attract, engage, and retain our workforce and do so in service of all stakeholders, not just shareholders. The pace of cultural, technological, and economic change demands it; we simply cannot stay the same as leaders and expect a different outcome.

Changing our priorities also demands a reframing of our relationship with the word "power." The evolving dynamics and demands in the workplace by employees, customers, and ecosystem partners require us to move away from the idea of power in the form of the "hero" leader, to one that is more democratized and emotionally mature. Power can no longer be thought of as a position based on hierarchy and organizational structure; rather, it is the responsibility that comes with inspiring and influencing people toward a shared vision and goal. Power, when focused on ideas of governance, stewardship, and the support of human flourishing, is leveraged softly. It is not a word representative of self-interest, control, and force, but of generosity, empowerment, and connection.

Ironically, research finds that people rise to positions of power due to their ability to exercise these soft skills – meaning their ability to empathize with others, display humility, and bring others into the decision-making process. Their power is exerted softly, which attracts others to follow them. Yet as soon as more power is obtained, these very same empathetic leaders lose their sense of others and instead focus on themselves. Social psychologist researcher Derchat Kelner coined the term *power paradox*, because it takes soft skills to obtain a true sense of lasting power and yet when that power is obtained, hard skills are then often leveraged.

The Cookie Monster Experiment

Consider this research experiment that continues to prove itself repeatedly. A team is huddled together in a conference room working on an assignment. There is a clear leader overseeing the group in the room and directing the process. An assistant walks into the room with a plate of cookies. There is one extra cookie on the plate. All members instinctively reach for a cookie and resume their work. But a strange thing occurs in the leader's behavior. They eat the cookie with their mouth open and spill crumbs on the table. Because this is a person in a position of power, no one says anything. There is one cookie left on the table. Without much thought or asking if anyone else wants it, the leader grabs the last cookie and continues to chew with their mouth open.

This research study has been named the cookie monster experiment. It summarizes the way people start to change once a position of power is obtained. They become blind to the needs of others and even stop adhering to basic social norms. And this power paradox carries over to more than just taking the last cookie. Further research shows that it's the wealthiest in America who shoplift the most. Those with higher power and more expensive cars are most likely to speed through a pedestrian zone with people in the walkway. Power and wealth tend to create blinders on leaders from seeing the needs of others. It is also why research has found that people in power are most inspired by their own stories and often lose interest when others start talking. This may explain why so many people in the workforce feel overlooked today. The power imbalance is deafening in many organizations as leaders become blind to those they are trying to lead.

So while power may start as soft, the power paradox warns that once power is obtained, many leaders lose sight of the very people who gave them that power to begin with. Dacher Keltner, professor of psychology at the University of California, Berkeley, states, "Our influence, the lasting difference that we make in the world, is ultimately only as good as what others think of us. Having enduring power is a privilege that depends on other people continuing to give it to us."[23] As a result, power based on hard skills may work for an amount of time, but that amount is finite. Power becomes infinite when we act in ways that improve other people's lives. Power is not forced upon others, but rather given to us through the essential soft skills that the workforce craves.

Thinking back to the examples of failed leadership in the beginning of this chapter, it may now be easy to see where things went wrong. These leaders rose to positions of power because of their ability to relate to others and their reputation for driving toward the common good. They failed fairly quickly because once power was obtained, they no longer worried about their reputation, nor how their actions impacted others. Instead, the ego took over and a more Machiavellian style of leadership occurred in their organizations. The result? Finite power that ended in a fairly public fall. Heeding these examples and overcoming the power paradox requires more than just good intentions and an understanding of what people need at work. It requires the new essentials of leadership that are grounded on a new way to think, behave, and ultimately lead.

9

The Essentials of Leadership

"A leader sees greatness in other people. You cannot be much of a leader if all you see is yourself."

—Maya Angelou[1]

The very nature of work is being redefined in our lifetime. Leadership is no longer marked by a position but rather by the way one engages and behaves – and it is on constant display. There is no hiding in the digital age, and the rising tension and friction between leaders and the workforce can no longer be ignored. In fact, trust is at an all-time low for leaders in organizations. In a Gallup survey in 2023, only 21% of US employees said they trust their leaders. Within this environment, issues that once resided outside corporate walls have become leadership imperatives, with the role of the leader transcending mere management into global citizenship. Consider that our youngest generation is entering the workforce already disillusioned and frustrated with leadership. Those in the US have grown up in a world where institutions have failed to protect them from gun violence in their schools, the effects of climate change, a global pandemic, or from witnessing political insurrection. As Dr. Elizabeth Sawin, director of Multisolving Institute, pointed out in a poignant social media post, these young people have "learned that they keep each other safe, and that having nothing change is scarier than change."[2] Frankly, there is no definitive playbook for how to meet this moment and restore trust – there are too many variables and co-dependencies to predict how the world will continue to transform with certainty – but if we are to leave the business world better than we found it, a new leadership model is required to steward our people through the vast change we will inevitably meet.

Jim Collins's Flywheel model, as introduced in his seminal book *Good to Great*, provides a compelling blueprint for such evolution, focusing on the cumulative power of consistent effort over time to generate significant outcomes. This is not the time for heroic efforts; it is the time for good leaders to rise to the occasion and start running businesses differently – one decision at a time – and to become emotionally mature leaders with the capacity to do good for others. The Flywheel model is not just a strategy but a philosophy that encapsulates the essence of momentum. It is a large, heavy wheel that takes a lot of effort to push. It begins moving slowly, but with persistence and effort the speed of the wheel increases exponentially due to the built-up energy. This model was developed through Collins's research, where he noticed that successful companies did not have dramatic breakthroughs or flamboyant leadership shifts, but rather they experienced a steady buildup of actions that advanced the companies' agendas, which he likened to a flywheel building momentum.

At its core, the Flywheel concept counters the quick-fix, results-oriented approach that often dominates the corporate landscape. Instead, it emphasizes a strategic sequence of actions that build upon each other, creating a cycle of reinforcing activities that drive each other forward. The key to this model is understanding that there are no overnight successes, but a gradual progression of decisions and improvements that collectively contribute to substantial achievements over time.

Why is this relevant to changing leadership behaviors? Traditional management often focuses on outcomes without considering the underlying forces shaping those outcomes. Leaders may push for results through top-down mandates or short-term incentives, ignoring the deeper cultural and operational shifts necessary for bringing humanity to the forefront of work. The Flywheel model shifts the focus from mere outcomes to the underlying processes that achieve these results, starting with mindset (see Figure 9.1).

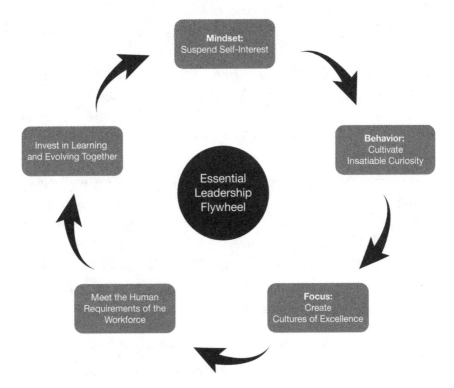

FIGURE 9.1 The essential leadership flywheel model.

Changing leadership behaviors using the Flywheel model involves rethinking the starting point of change initiatives. Instead of beginning with desired outcomes, it begins with the leadership's mindset – their beliefs, values, and assumptions about what drives success. Leaders must cultivate a mindset that values incremental progress, celebrates small wins, and understands the compound effect of sustained efforts. This mindset then translates into consistent behaviors that contribute to the gradual acceleration of the flywheel. Finally, the momentum generated from these leadership behaviors results in deeper organization-wide transformation, changing the way the company operates. Getting the flywheel started by meeting the essentials of what people need at work does not come overnight. But with continued development on leadership change, the momentum created can truly affect the way leaders lead and the impact they have on others.

As will be discovered, the Essential Leadership Flywheel is about transforming the very nature of how companies operate, and leaders think. It is a vital shift from a results-oriented to a process-oriented mindset that focuses as much on the *how* as the *what* within a business. And it works because it elevates the leader's orientation toward emotional maturity. Emotional maturity is leaders' capacity to see and understand themselves in service of seeing, understanding, and connecting with those sitting across from them. The concept moves beyond emotional intelligence because it is actionable and relational. It defines the kind of leader that the workforce, and the world, is desperately asking for. To become an emotionally mature, essential leader, the kind who can activate the momentum of an entire flywheel within an organization, requires three core elements:

- Essential leadership mindset: Suspend self-interest.
- Essential leadership behavior: Cultivate insatiable curiosity.
- Essential leadership focus: Create cultures of excellence.

The success of the flywheel depends on leaders' ability to activate these essential skills and ways of operating in their daily work. It is only through their adoption that they can set out to meet the human requirements of their workforce as outlined in Part II and successfully leverage the power of human intelligence to work alongside AI effectively and innovatively. These essentials of human-powered leadership are the key to business transformation and the future of work.

Suspend Self-Interest

Researchers long ago discovered that the way we ultimately behave is driven by the way we think.[3] Mindsets matter a lot when it comes to leadership. We know that the power paradox often blinds leaders from thinking or even being aware of the needs of others. The question is, How can you overcome the power paradox to get momentum started in the flywheel? Many leaders seek more productivity and innovation within their organizations, and yet few realize that it starts with themselves. The greatest inhibitor to driving workforce performance is a leader's own ego and relentless pursuit of shorter-term gains that benefit the top of the organization, often on the backs of those very workers they are seeking to motivate. This is why getting the flywheel going is so highly dependent on its very first step: the suspension of self-interest.

Suspension of self-interest means more than simply being aware of your own emotional state, which is important but not enough. It takes self-awareness a step further by requiring leaders to extend their boundaries in service of others – when a team member, a customer, or a partner needs help, attention, or grace. To be clear, this mindset is not about ignoring your own feelings or well-being and putting others first at all costs – ruinous empathy, as CEO coach Kim Scott calls it. It is about investing focused time and attention in others to truly understand and honor their needs; it requires you to set aside ego and the limitations that it puts on the depth of your human interactions. The suspension of self-interest is about being able to respond effectively and meaningfully, rather than react based on personal interest and partiality to the people and groups to whom you are accountable.

In an era where short-term gains are often pursued at the expense of long-term sustainability, leaders who transcend their own interests to champion their people and the broader organizational goals are increasingly vital. The stories of Paul Polman at Unilever and Satya Nadella at Microsoft exemplify how selfless leadership not only steers corporations toward great humancentric practices but also drives significant business success.

Paul Polman redefined strategic focus at Unilever with an unrelenting commitment to sustainability that was, at the time, both revolutionary and risky. When he took over as CEO in 2009, Polman immediately eliminated quarterly reporting to shareholders – a bold move meant to shift the focus from short-term profits to long-term sustainable growth. This shift in focus from short-term profits – which often benefit CEOs in the form of bonuses and reputation boosts for their quick wins – to long-term sustainability and ethical practices is an example of suspended self-interest in action. It was far less about personal gains than it was about setting the company up for future success, even beyond Polman's tenure.

Under his guidance, Unilever also launched the Unilever Sustainable Living Plan, aiming to decouple business growth from environmental impact, a strategy that significantly realigned the company's operations. In this context, suspending self-interest meant putting the needs of broader stakeholders – including employees, customers, and global communities – above personal or corporate short-term financial benefits. This aligns with a more holistic view of the company's role in society, which can sometimes be at odds with the financial expectations of share-holders. This focus on sustainable and ethical practices did not diminish Unilever's profitability; instead, the company thrived, demonstrating that long-term, values-driven business strategies can lead to superior financial returns.

Similarly, Satya Nadella's leadership transformation at Microsoft pivoted the company culture from competitiveness to collaboration and creativity. Upon becoming CEO in 2014, Nadella championed a "learn-it-all" culture over a "know-it-all" culture, focusing on empathy, learning, and development. This shift was not merely cosmetic but was embedded deeply into the operational practices and business strategies of Microsoft. Under Nadella's leadership, Microsoft not only increased its market value, crossing the $1 trillion threshold but also reinvigorated its global influence and innovative capacity. His approach to foster-ing an inclusive and growth-oriented culture proved critical in revitalizing Microsoft's image and operations.

Both leaders showcase the profound impact of prioritizing employee-centered policies and stakeholder needs over personal gain or immediate financial metrics. Their strategies demonstrate a clear link between selfless leadership and high organizational performance. Research supports this correlation; a study in the *Journal of Business Ethics* found that selfless leadership practices enhance job satisfaction and boost organizational commitment and performance.[4] Decades of academic research also notes that leaders who engage in self-sacrificing behavior are perceived as more inspirational and more effective by the people they lead, which resonates through higher employee engagement and loy-alty.[5] These leaders understand that by setting aside personal interests to focus on more significant, collective goals, they cre-ate a ripple effect of motivation and commitment throughout their organizations. The momentum in the flywheel begins only when leaders think and behave in a manner that clearly suspends suspicion of self-interest in behavior.

To suspend one's own self-interest in service of the team or an individual requires an examination of our motivations when interacting within an organization. Clearly, we as leaders need to do the job we were hired for and fulfill our employee contract – no one disputes this reality. How we do this depends on our personal motivators: Are we motivated by our own financial or personal gains? Does it serve our ego and sense of self-importance? Or are we motivated by doing our work with our team's and others' success in mind?

The leadership exemplified by figures like Polman and Nadella is not just admirable but essential for today's businesses aiming to navigate the complexities of today's work environment. Their legacies underscore that true leadership success is measured not by personal accolades but by the ability to inspire entire organizations toward broader, altruistic goals. As the business landscape continues to evolve, the call for leaders to transcend personal interests in favor of nurturing resilient, innovative, and ethical organizations will only grow louder.

Suspending self-interest is the critical first step in the Flywheel model to generate momentum and inspire a workforce to contribute to its energy. For leaders who want to take this step and drive meaningful change, here are a few clear actions to consider:

- **Prioritize daily reflection.** Reflective practices involve a deliberate process of self-examination and critical thinking about one's actions, decisions, and leadership style. For leaders, engaging in reflective practices means taking the time to step back from the immediacy of daily tasks to contemplate their behaviors, the outcomes of their decisions, and the dynamics they create within their teams. This introspective process is essential for continuous personal and professional growth and for fostering a deep understanding of how one's leadership impacts others. It also allows a longer-term focus to become clearer and enables the broader system to come into view.

- **Cultivate a relentless focus on others.** In an era where distractions abound, the act of fully engaging with another person is becoming a lost art, particularly in high-pressure environments. The proliferation of meditation apps signals a widespread challenge in maintaining focus. Leaders must demonstrate an ironclad commitment to their teams by actively removing distractions in interactions. This involves turning off digital devices during meetings, establishing clear "do not disturb" protocols, and prioritizing the human connection above all. By doing so, leaders not only make their team members feel valued but also set a standard for what genuine engagement should look like within the organization.

- **Root out office politics.** Office politics are not just a petty annoyance; they are a culture killer. According to a *Financial Times* article titled "Office politics is not optional: Learn to play the game or you'll be its victim," the manipulative tactics involved in office politics can significantly dampen employee engagement and contribute to a toxic work environment. The author, Miranda Green, starts the piece with "If there is one thing people seem to hate more than politics, it's office politics. Backstabbing, conniving, sucking up and kicking down: being on career-enhancing maneuvers makes people the target of derision among colleagues."[6]

  Leaders must take a hard stance against such behaviors by promoting a culture of transparency and meritocracy. It's imperative to dismantle the structures that support self-serving schemes and replace them with systems that reward genuine merit and collaborative success. Only through such radical honesty can a leader inspire true loyalty and drive team performance. Playing politics is in service of one thing: a leader's ego or personal agenda. When power is at the center of one's agenda and ego, the motivation becomes climbing the proverbial "corporate ladder," which leaves no room for others unless they serve the leader's purpose. People become the means to a personal end.

- **Foster a culture of open communication and feedback.** Suspending self-interest is non-negotiable in leadership, and doing so requires the input of others in order to see yourself as you are seen by others. Ironically, the level of upward feedback is often restricted the higher up you go within an organization. So leaders must not only invite but insist on regular, open communication channels with their teams. This means scheduling frequent forums – weekly, monthly, or at least quarterly – where employees can openly discuss what's working, what's not, and how the leadership can better support them. Importantly, these meetings must occur without fear of retribution and with a genuine openness from leaders to act on the feedback received. As noted by *Harvard Business Review* in 2016, fostering such open dialogue is critical for leaders looking to build trust and adaptability within their teams.[7]

Cultivate Insatiable Curiosity

When was the last time you read a book that you could not put down or watched a TV show that you felt compelled to binge? We all know that feeling of wonder: the excitement about what's going to happen next, the pull of good storytelling, and the attachment to characters you love or hate. These experiences are defined by complete immersion – everything else fades away. This is what it's like to be insatiably curious. Every person has a story that deserves that same kind of attention and wonder. It is the foundation of relationship building, and emotionally mature leaders are experts at drawing out the stories that other people want to share with them. Making the space and time to engage this way defines the job of the leader.

Being insatiably curious starts with a simple "hello" and a meaningful "How are you?" It is about creating a safe space to get to know your employees. In an age when trust and engagement are at an all-time low, listening is an undervalued and essential skill. No matter what level a leader is within an organization or how much time they have, it is their responsibility to make the time and create the conditions for meaningful connection.

Insatiable curiosity is not just beneficial for leaders – it's essential. Yet many leaders fall short, engaging with their teams only during formal evaluations or when problems arise. This shortfall is often pronounced in diverse environments, where leaders might shy away from deep interactions due to discomfort or fear of missteps. This absence of curiosity and failure to suspend self-interest is a critical failure in leadership and undermines the potential for growth and connection. To continue the momentum of the flywheel, one must prioritize understanding and engagement with team members regularly, not just when performance metrics are due.

Sir Richard Branson, the visionary founder of the Virgin Group, exemplifies how a leader's profound curiosity, stemming from an unselfish commitment to others, can create transformative connections with both customers and employees. His entrepreneurial journey is distinguished by an insatiable curiosity and a relentless drive to redefine the norms of customer and employee engagement. His hands-on, democratic approach to leadership – regularly engaging with employees at all levels, fostering a culture of openness, and actively soliciting their input – does more than gather insights. It signals a respect and appreciation for the team that drives the conglomerate's success, fostering a deeply loyal and motivated workforce. Branson's success in building a highly effective team isn't the result of some environmental change to boost productivity, but rather the effect of someone taking the time to listen and respond to what they needed.

Moreover, when Branson launched Virgin Atlantic, his motivation extended far beyond traditional business metrics; he aimed to revolutionize the air travel experience. His initiatives, such as introducing the premium economy class and offering unique in-flight services like onboard massages, were groundbreaking responses to customer needs, sourced from his direct interactions and deep empathy with passengers. This wasn't just innovation for profit's sake – it was a deliberate effort to enhance the human aspect of air travel, making it more enjoyable and accessible.

Of course, Branson's venture into the final frontier with Virgin Galactic goes beyond mere business expansion. It is driven by a vision to connect with the universal human ambition of space exploration. Branson's move to make space travel attainable for non-astronauts showcases his commitment to expanding the horizons of ordinary people, demonstrating a profound understanding of and respect for the wider aspirations of humanity.

Richard Branson's leadership illustrates how a leader's deep-seated curiosity about and dedication to serving the needs and dreams of others can catalyze industry-wide innovation. His unrelenting focus on humanizing business and investing in genuine relationships has not only created loyal followings among consumers and employees alike but has also solidified his legacy as a pioneer who redefines the boundaries of entrepreneurial leadership.

For leaders who want to take the next step in the Flywheel concept to become insatiably curious and drive meaningful change, here are few clear actions to consider:

- **Get to know your human workforce – in detail.** The first rule of being insatiably curious is that it's not about you, it is about getting to know the human or team you are engaging with. We tend to overcomplicate what it means to be insatiably curious: It is simply a desire to understand more about your people and the teams that work with you. It is about asking good questions and listening intently in order to ask even better follow-up questions. Do not be afraid to inquire: What's really going on? Or simply say, "Tell me more." Getting to know your colleagues and teams means making the time, building it into your calendar, and silencing all distractions – phones, smart watches, email alerts – to focus on learning about whom you are interacting with, as if your life depended on it.

  Part of getting to know your workforce includes understanding what motivates them; that includes what your team members love about their work and in their lives. The opportunity for leaders here is to create pathways for employees to see the connections between their own passions and interests and the company's purpose. These days, we know that many people join organizations because of mission and values, but only one in six people report feeling highly connected to their organization. Moreover, a mere one in five feel comfortable sharing problems or conflicts at work, and one in four believe their leaders are responsive to their needs or communicate regularly.[8] This is a breakdown of belonging and connection.

While getting to know your team and colleagues is not necessarily complicated, it is not always easy given the productivity pressures placed on managers and leaders. But an emotionally mature leader has the courage to set a new standard and reprioritize the way we work to those ends. They create more opportunities for connection and make an effort to build greater understanding between each other beyond tasks and roles we play.

- **Sculpt workplaces where passion and profession intersect.** In his insightful book *Love + Work*, Marcus Buckingham articulates a truth many find in their professional journey: no job is perfect, and it's rare to love every aspect of your work. However, Buckingham highlights a potent opportunity within this reality – the daily pursuit of moments that ignite our passion. Finding a fulfilling career is not about a utopian job that fulfills every desire, but identifying those gems of activity, interaction, or achievement that resonate deeply with us each day.

  Leaders play a pivotal role in this process. They have the capability, and responsibility, not only to discover what their team members are passionate about but also to actively integrate these passions into the everyday fabric of their work. The challenge and art lie in aligning an individual's love with their daily tasks and the broader organizational goals.

  Take, for example, a leader in a tech company who notices that one of her software developers lights up when discussing user interface design more so than the other aspects of his job. Recognizing this, the leader might arrange for this developer to take a lead role in the UI/UX aspect of upcoming projects. Furthermore, they could facilitate mentorship opportunities with senior designers or provide resources for advanced training in graphic design. This not only enhances the developer's job satisfaction by aligning his tasks with his interests, but also benefits the organization by fostering a culture of engagement and innovation.

As we explored in Chapter 7, leaders must initiate regular, meaningful dialogs with their employees to unearth these interests. This could be through one-on-one meetings, team workshops, or even informal conversations. The key is to create a space where employees feel comfortable expressing what truly motivates them without the fear of judgment or reprisal.

In cultivating this environment, leaders help bridge the gap between personal passions and mere work tasks. This alignment is essential for combating workplace disengagement and building a trust-rich organizational culture. This is especially true as the workforce becomes more fluid and more of it derives from freelance populations. When people see that their leaders care about their interests and are committed to integrating them into their work, it not only boosts morale but also loyalty and productivity. Thus, the leader's role transcends managing workflows or projects; it becomes about fostering a community where work is a source of fulfillment and joy.

- **Create communities of practice.** One of our favorite leadership consultants is Margaret Wheatley, who after nearly six decades of practice has come to this conclusion: "Wherever there is a problem, community is the answer." For leaders acting from a place of insatiable curiosity, creating communities is essential to learning firsthand from broader stakeholders. Often, the miss here is that leaders treat their communities as if they are disjointed from the work itself, believing that while developing communities around shared interests may help cultivate connection, supporting business-adjacent community building does not ultimately make a significant impact on their company. But consider the story of Apple.

Tim Cook brought in Angela Ahrendts, former CEO of Burberry, to lead Apple's retail business in 2014. From the outset, Apple's retail strategy focused on creating spaces to foster community interaction. This vision was clear when the first Apple Store opened in 2001 in Tysons Corner, Virginia. Steve Jobs, Apple's co-founder, intended for the stores to be more than just sales floors; he envisioned them as community spaces that engage customers with the brand and each other.[9] Ahrendts helped Apple further bring this vision to life by transforming its stores into community hubs where technology meets lifestyle. She redesigned the stores to function as modern-day town squares: a place where people naturally meet up and spend time.[10] In this way, the Apple Store became not merely a place to purchase products, but a venue where customers come to learn, explore, and connect with others. This innovative approach to retail significantly enhanced customer loyalty and transformed the shopping experience.

One of the key features of Apple Stores that facilitate this community building is the architecture, design of the open floor plan, and accessibility to products, services, and employees alike. A central point of the stores of course became the Genius Bar – a tech support station within the stores where customers can not only troubleshoot their devices, but interact with knowledgeable staff in a welcoming, noncorporate environment. The setup not only resolves technical issues but also fosters a sense of belonging among

Apple users. Moreover, Apple introduced various programs aimed at enriching community interaction. For instance, "Today at Apple" sessions, which began in 2017, are free educational events available in Apple Stores worldwide. These sessions cover a wide range of topics, from art and design to coding and photography, led by professionals in the field. The idea is to create a space where customers can come together to learn new skills, often using Apple products, thereby enhancing their engagement with the brand while connecting with fellow attendees.

Most critically, Ahrendts's success in fulfilling Jobs's vision for Apple's retail stores stemmed from a deep understanding that the foundation of community starts with how you cultivate relationships with employees: "Everyone talks about building a relationship with your customer. I think you build one with your employees first."[11]

Christie had the great privilege and pleasure to work alongside Ahrendts during her time at the company and witnessed firsthand the profound impact this emotionally mature leader had on her teams and in the broader organization. Ahrendts prioritized spending concentrated time with retail employees, whom she met with intense curiosity, respect, and a laser focus on listening to their experience and ideas for the stores. Her effect on Apple's culture of belonging, purpose, and agency was profound.

At its core, the impact of this community-oriented approach engendered trust among Apple's customer base by first establishing it internally with employees. Angela's leadership style exemplifies the idea of a company's "insides matching their outsides." She once said, "When you have trust in place throughout the company, people are empowered, people are free."[12] Putting humans at the center and building trust is still evident in Apple's stores today, enhancing customer satisfaction by providing a richer, more interactive shopping experience and, more broadly, building strong brand loyalty. Customers associate Apple not just with products, but with enjoyable and enriching social experiences.

Create Cultures of Excellence

As the Essential Leadership Flywheel model begins to gain momentum through a leader's suspension of self-interest and insatiable curiosity, it then turns outward toward the broader organization. Leaders must now consider how to share this momentum with the rest of the company to create a culture of excellence through its shared humanity. A culture of excellence within an organization transcends the mere setting of high standards; it is about putting words into action and a leader's courage to face the winds of today's constant change and adversity head on in how they build and operate. This approach is what builds resilience within teams when challenges arise and the path forward is unclear, as it is for many leaders today trying to figure out a world defined by global shifts, rapid technological advancement, and new working models. Leaders who pursue cultures of excellence build not just strong companies, but strong communities who lean on their purpose, values, and sense of connection with each other to navigate this change. They empower team members to view obstacles as opportunities for growth and learning, rather than roadblocks to success. This is because the same mindset is modeled by their leadership day in and day out. It's one thing to have momentum when you have tailwinds; it's another thing entirely when your workforce faces headwinds.

Cultures of excellence reflect the hard work of leaders who invest in the very best of our human qualities, ultimately fueling creativity, teamwork, and innovation. As a result of this investment, our organizations will continuously evolve in response to changing market dynamics and internal feedback, always striving for improvement, and prioritizing long-term sustainability in their practices. A culture of excellence ensures the flywheel keeps spinning, regardless of the external forces it faces because its leaders continue to consistently recommit their energy to moving it forward.

Consider Arne Sorenson, the late CEO of Marriott International. Sorenson, who led Marriott from 2012 until his passing in 2021, was particularly adept at navigating complex global contexts while maintaining a focus on meeting the needs of the company's expansive workforce.

Under Sorenson's leadership, Marriott expanded significantly, including the major acquisition of Starwood Hotels & Resorts in 2016, which made Marriott the world's largest hotel chain. Despite the complexities and potential disruptions from such a large merger, Sorenson successfully integrated the companies by prioritizing a culture that valued every employee's contribution, recognizing the diverse backgrounds and perspectives they brought to the table. Any leader who has undergone M&A work knows how difficult the culture transformation piece can be when merging two distinct ways of working together.

Sorenson, who was known for his deep commitment to diversity, equity, and inclusion, believed these were not just moral imperatives but strategic business advantages that created a culture of excellence. He championed programs for employee development, career advancement opportunities, and initiatives aimed at increasing the representation of women and minorities in leadership roles. He was also an outspoken advocate for public issues, including standing against legislation that was discriminatory toward LGBTQ+ individuals.

Additionally, during the COVID-19 pandemic, Sorenson made heartfelt communications to employees, highlighting the company's challenges while also expressing his commitment to workforce safety and job security. His empathetic leadership during this crisis helped to maintain trust and morale among the workforce, reinforcing a culture of mutual support and resilience. Sorenson's approach to leadership at Marriott exemplified how a deep understanding of the diverse contexts of a global workforce and a commitment to inclusivity can drive a company not only to achieve operational excellence but also to nurture a positive, ethical, and inclusive work environment.

Fostering cultures of excellence is the next critical step in the Flywheel model to generate momentum and inspire a workforce, regardless of what's happening more broadly around them. For leaders who want to take this step and operate with excellence, here are few clear actions to consider:

- **Practice contextual competency**. The one thing that set Sorenson apart was his contextual competency. This ability to understand and adapt to various contexts – what we term as "contextual competency" – is crucial. This skill involves leaders expanding their own boundaries to recognize and appreciate the context in which their team members operate. This understanding not only facilitates effective communication and decision-making but also fosters a resilient, supportive work environment capable of weathering hardships.

  Contextual competency enables leaders to discern the subtle, often unspoken aspects of their team's dynamics, industry specifics, and socioeconomic conditions impacting their work. This capability is especially critical when the essential leadership flywheel faces the inevitable frictions caused by misalignments or misunderstandings arising from differing contexts. As M. Scott Peck eloquently puts it in *The Road Less Traveled*, acknowledging that "life is difficult" is a steppingstone toward dealing with life's complexities.

This recognition is essential for leaders, because the difficulties encountered by their teams often stem from unique and challenging circumstances that must be understood and addressed to maintain the flywheel's momentum.

Understanding another's context involves more than just empathy; it requires an active and ongoing effort to learn about and engage with the different realities that affect team members' performance and well-being. For instance, a leader might consider the impact of cultural backgrounds on team interaction, the personal challenges employees face outside of work, or even the broader economic issues that shape industry conditions. Each of these elements can introduce friction into the flywheel, slowing progress and dampening morale.

Leaders who excel in contextual competency are adept at adjusting their strategies to better align with the realities of their team's situation. This might mean altering project timelines, providing additional support and resources, or modifying expectations to better suit the real-world challenges the team faces. For example, during the COVID-19 pandemic, leaders who quickly understood the drastically altered contexts of their employees' lives – such as remote work challenges, health fears, and family responsibilities – were better equipped to make necessary adjustments that maintained productivity and team cohesion.

Scholarly research supports the importance of contextual competency in leadership. According to Mansour Javidan and colleagues, who discuss global leadership effectiveness in their article "A Whole New Global Mindset for Leadership,"[13] understanding the influence of national culture and industry conditions on organizational behavior is pivotal for leaders operating in international contexts. They argue that leaders who ignore these contextual differences are likely to encounter resistance and inefficiency, underscoring the broader applicability of contextual understanding across various leadership scenarios.

Further, contextual competency is not a static skill but a dynamic one that requires continual development. Leaders must commit to lifelong learning, actively seeking out opportunities to engage with different perspectives and new experiences that broaden their understanding of the diverse contexts in which their teams operate. This is why the suspension of self-interest and insatiable curiosity are prerequisites in the flywheel. You are unable to develop contextual competency without them.

Ultimately, by developing contextual competency, leaders not only mitigate the friction that can stop the leadership flywheel but also enhance their team's capacity to deal with adversity. This proactive approach to leadership ensures that the pursuit of excellence is a sustainable endeavor, characterized by resilience and adaptability in the face of challenges. Such leaders are better prepared to maintain momentum and drive their organizations toward long-term success, embodying the principle that truly effective leadership is about expanding one's boundaries to foster a deeper connection and understanding within their teams.

- **Understand the concept of culture as multidimensional.** Culture exists in organizations on the organizational, team, and individual level. It's essential to understand that company culture is inherently nuanced and multidimensional, reflecting the complexity and diversity of the environments in which we operate. At the highest level, culture is framed by the core principles that define our organization's mission and the values that guide how we create value and interact with our stakeholders. This strategic framing is crucial because it sets the tone for every other aspect of the organization. And it's needed. Research found that only 41% of US employees know what their company stands for and how it's different from its competitors.[14]

Moving from the enterprise to the team level, culture becomes more operational. It is at this juncture that the high-level principles are interpreted and applied in ways that align with specific team goals and dynamics. Each team, depending on its unique function, location, and composition, may require a different approach to embody these overarching principles effectively. An article from the *Harvard Business Review* on implementing hybrid work models highlights this point by discussing how companies that tailored their approach to fit the specific circumstances of different teams saw improved outcomes in both productivity and employee satisfaction.[15]

The individual dimension of culture is where personal identity within the organization takes shape. Employees ask themselves, "Who am I in relation to this organization?" This question is crucial for individual engagement with the organizational culture at large. Each member of the organization constructs their identity at work based on how they perceive and experience the company's values lived out in their day-to-day activities. Employees find alignment between their own professional goals and behaviors with what they observe and feel on the team and organizational levels, without having to sacrifice their individuality. By that we mean that a person's role in company culture should never be about denying their own sense of self and values to fit in or succeed; it is about finding how they can uniquely contribute to carrying out an organization's purpose and values in their daily work and interactions.

As leaders, it's vital to cultivate a culture that resonates on all these levels – enterprise, team, and individual. At the enterprise level, clearly articulate the foundational principles that define who we are and how we operate. At the team level, empower leaders to adapt these principles to the team's specific needs, creating a more responsive and effective working environment. And at the individual level, encourage a culture of introspection and personal growth, where employees can align their personal values with those of the organization in a way that is true to their own identity.

By acknowledging and nurturing these multiple dimensions of culture, we create a more cohesive, dynamic, and successful organization where everyone feels valued and understood. This approach not only enhances performance but also fosters a workplace where people are genuinely connected to their work and to each other.

A Call to Leaders

We stand at the crossroads of business and cultural evolution, and the call to action for leaders has never been clearer: We must integrate radical humanity into our workplace practices if we are to make progress within our organizations and outside of them. Humanity itself is not in need of fixing – humanity needs good leadership. We must recenter its critical role in our business success and our health and fulfillment as a people. We must revolutionize the way we work to improve the way we *all* live. It is time to make space for and invest in the development and celebration of humanity at work.

The concept of the Essential Leadership Flywheel – continuously driving and improving our own practices – presents us not just with a model for leadership, but with a strategy for putting people back at the heart of our work. This is more than an operational necessity; it is a moral imperative that places humanity itself at stake.

Leaders, we live in a world that is currently defined by upheaval, change, ambiguity, and anxiety about the future. Now is the time to embrace this challenge. We must foster environments where human intelligence is valued as greatly as technological advancement – to recognize that they are inextricably linked and that without the former, the latter will fail to reach its full potential. *We must honor our people by recognizing that purpose, agency, well-being, and connection are not just encouraged, but required for the future of business.* It is in these environments that workers thrive, innovation flourishes, and organizational goals are met with unprecedented success. Our approach to leadership should not merely be about managing resources but about nurturing human potential – acknowledging the personal and professional motivations and aspirations of every individual through our ability to suspend self-interest, practice curiosity, and build cultures of excellence.

This moment calls for a bold reimagining of what leadership itself looks like. It demands leaders who are not only visionaries but also humanitarians – leaders who recognize that every policy, every strategy, and every decision has profound human implications. We must commit to a leadership model that views the workforce not as a series of inputs into a system but as a vibrant community of essential individuals, each with unique needs, dreams, and challenges.

As we use the flywheel to propel our organizations forward, let us also use it to advance a culture of inclusivity, understanding, and compassion. Let this be the legacy of our time in leadership: that we were the ones who stood up for humanity in the workplace, who recognized that our greatest asset was not our products or services, but how we impact people. This is not just a responsibility – it is the business imperative of our time. As Margaret Mead, a cultural anthropologist, noted, "Never doubt that a small group of thoughtful, concerned citizens can change the world. Indeed, it is the only thing that ever has." The only difference? As leaders, we are not only a small group of citizens; we have the unique opportunity to leverage our privilege and power for the greater good if we stand together to change the status quo.

Now is the moment. If we fail to integrate these essentials of leadership, we risk losing not just the hearts and minds of our people, but the very essence of what makes our organizations excel and buzz with potential. Let us rise to this occasion and redefine what it means to lead by centering humanity in every decision we make. Let us build not just companies, but communities of excellence that reflect our highest ideals and aspirations. This is our call to action, for the sake of humanity and the future we are all a part of shaping.

Endnotes

Introduction

1. "Work Innovators Drive the Success of AI-Enabled Organizations," November 2, 2023, https://www.upwork.com/research/work-innovator-report/2023
2. Pendell, Ryan. "Employee Engagement Strategies: Fixing the World's $8.8 Trillion Problem," Gallup.Com, September 11, 2023, https://www.gallup.com/workplace/393497/world-trillion-workplace-problem.aspx

Chapter 1

1. "30 Quotes About Trust That Will Make You Think," https://www.inc.com/lolly-daskal/trust-me-these-30-quotes-about-trust-could-make-a-huge-difference.html
2. "UPS Workers Approve New Contract with Hard-fought Pay and Safety Wins, Ending Strike Threat," NBC News, August 22, 2023, https://www.nbcnews.com/business/business-news/ups-workers-approve-new-contract-hard-fought-pay-safety-gains-rcna100466
3. Wren, D.A., and Bedeian, A.G. (2009). *The Evolution of Management Thought*, 6e. New York: Wiley.
4. Ibid.
5. Chandler, A.D. (1956). *Henry Varnum Poor: Business Editor, Analyst and Reformer*. Cambridge, MA: Harvard University Press.
6. Williams, Whiting. (1920). *What Workers Want*.
7. Boyer, P.S. (ed.) (2001). *The Oxford Companion to United States History*. New York: Oxford University Press.
8. Wood, J.C., and Michael C.W. (eds.) (2003). *Henry Ford: Critical Evaluations in Business and Management. Volume 1*. London: Routledge.

9. Wilson, D.D. (1916). "Halting the Taylor System," *Machinist Monthly Journal* 23 (11): 1107–1108.
10. Roethlisberger, F.J., and Dickson, W.J. (1939). *Management and the Worker*. Cambridge, MA: Havard University Press.
11. "Appreciation for a System: The W. Edwards Deming Institute," W. Edwards Deming Institute, n.d., https://deming.org/appreciation-for-a-system
12. Baker, Wayne. (2020). *All You Have to Do Is Ask: How to Master the Most Important Skill for Success*. New York: Penguin Random House.
13. Foss, Nicolai J., and Klein, Peter G. "Rethinking Hierarchy," *MIT Sloan Management Review*, January 25, 2023, https://sloanreview.mit.edu/article/rethinking-hierarchy
14. Cross, Rob, Reb Rebele, and Adam Grant, "Collaborative Overload," *Harvard Business Review*, January–February 2016, https://hbr.org/2016/01/collaborative-overload
15. "What Google Learned from Its Quest to Build the Perfect Team," *New York Times*, February 28, 2016, https://www.nytimes.com/2016/02/28/magazine/what-google-learned-from-its-quest-to-build-the-perfect-team.html
16. Edmondson, A.C. (1999). "Psychological Safety and Learning Behavior in Work Teams," *Administrative Science Quarterly* 44 (2): 350–383, https://doi.org/10.2307/2666999
17. Ocean Tomo, "Intangible Asset Market Value Study," March 30, 2022, https://oceantomo.com/intangible-asset-market-value-study
18. Davenport, Thomas H. "When Jobs Become Commodities," *MIT Sloan Management Review*, July 21, 2017, https://sloanreview.mit.edu/article/when-jobs-become-commodities
19. Estrada, Sheryl. "'Skills are the currency of the future': The rise of a skills-based economy," HR Dive, November 5, 2020, https://www.hrdive.com/news/skills-currency-future-skills-based-economy/588475

Chapter 2

1. Aneesh Raman and Maria Flynn, "When Your Technical Skills Are Eclipsed, Your Humanity Will Matter More Than Ever," *New York Times*, February 14, 2024, https://www.nytimes.com/2024/02/14/opinion/ai-economy-jobs-colleges.html
2. "Talent Shortage," n.d., https://go.manpowergroup.com/talent-shortage
3. Greg Smith, "Work Is Changing, Again. Here's How to Thrive in the Skills Economy," *Forbes*, April 26, 2022, https://www.forbes.com/sites/forbestechcouncil/2022/04/25/work-is-changing-again-heres-how-to-thrive-in-the-skills-economy/?sh=5f5876974944
4. https://www.kornferry.com/insights/this-week-in-leadership/talent-crunch-future-of-work

5. "Beyond Hiring: How Companies Are Reskilling to Address Talent Gaps," McKinsey & Company, February 12, 2020, https://www.mckinsey .com/capabilities/people-and-organizational-performance/our-insights/ beyond-hiring-how-companies-are-reskilling-to-address-talent-gaps

6. "The Future of Jobs Report 2023," World Economic Forum, n.d., https://www.weforum.org/publications/the-future-of-jobs-report-2023/ in-full/4-skills-outlook

7. Annie Brown, "AI Is Not Going to Replace Writers Anytime Soon – but the Future Might Be Closer Than You Think," *Forbes*, October 10, 2023, https://www.forbes.com/sites/anniebrown/2021/07/20/ai-is-not-going-to-replace-writers-anytime-soon--but-the-future-might-be-closer-than-you-think/?sh=5b7930df6087

8. "Blue Collar Jobs with the Lowest Risk of Automation," Industrial Equipment News, September 7, 2023, https://www.ien.com/automation/ article/22872005/blue-collar-jobs-with-the-lowest-risk-of-automation

9. "How Land O'Lakes Is Cultivating Ag-tech to Help Farmers Harvest Healthier Profits," Source, May 9, 2023, https://news.microsoft.com/source/ features/digital-transformation/how-land-o-lakes-cultivating-agriculture-tech-help-farmers-harvest-healthier-profits

10. Debra Sabatini Hennelly, "Bridging Generational Divides in Your Workplace," *Harvard Business Review*, January 10, 2023, https://hbr .org/2023/01/bridging-generational-divides-in-your-workplace

11. "The Baby Boomer Effect and Controlling Healthcare Costs, USC EMHA Online," n.d., https://healthadministrationdegree.usc.edu/blog/ the-baby-boomer-effect-and-controlling-health-care-costs

12. Alyssa Fowers and Kevin Schaul, "How the Graying of America Is Reshaping the Workforce and Economy," *Washington Post*, July 1, 2023, https://www .washingtonpost.com/technology/interactive/2023/aging-america-retirees-workforce-economy

13. Taryn Netzer, "Baby Boomers Retiring, Leaving Many Open Trades Positions," *Industrial Safety & Hygiene News*, November 17, 2023, https:// www.ishn.com/articles/110888-baby-boomers-retiring-leaving-many-open-trades-positions

14. Brian Ballou, "Survey Shows Gen X and Baby Boomers Have Not Warmed Up to AI," Techstrong.ai, September 21, 2023, https://techstrong .ai/articles/survey-shows-gen-x-and-baby-boomers-have-not-warmed-up-to-ai/#:~:text=The%20study%20suggests%20that%20baby,their%20 lives%2C%2040%25%20aren

15. Joanna Barsh et al., "Unlocking the Full Potential of Women in the U.S. Economy," 2011, https://www.wsj.com/public/resources/documents/ WSJExecutiveSummary.pdf

16. Janet L. Yellen, "The History of Women's Work and Wages and How It Has Created Success for Us All," Brookings, May 7, 2020, https://www .brookings.edu/articles/the-history-of-womens-work-and-wages-and-how-it-has-created-success-for-us-all

17. "Working Women: Data From the Past, Present and Future," Department of Labor Blog, March 15, 2023, https://blog.dol.gov/2023/03/15/working-women-data-from-the-past-present-and-future

18. https://www.uschamber.com/workforce/understanding-americas-labor-shortage

19. https://www.mckinsey.com/capabilities/people-and-organizational-performance/our-insights/unlocking-the-full-potential-of-women

20. Stephanie Ferguson and Isabella Lucy, "Data Deep Dive: A Decline of Women in the Workforce," US Chamber of Commerce, April 27, 2022, https://www.uschamber.com/workforce/data-deep-dive-a-decline-of-women-in-the-workforce

21. "Women Were Awarded More PhDs in the US Than Men Last Year," World Economic Forum, February 7, 2020, https://www.weforum.org/agenda/2018/10/chart-of-the-day-more-women-than-men-earned-phds-in-the-us-last-year

22. "Glassdoor's 2024 Workplace Trends: Glassdoor Economic Research,"n.d., https://www.glassdoor.com/research/workplace-trends-2024#Trend1

23. "Workforce analysis and insights that empower leaders," UKG Workforce Institute, n.d., https://workforceinstitute.org

24. "The Skills Gap Is so Big That Nearly Half of Workers Will Need to Retrain This Decade," *Fortune*, May 1, 2023, https://fortune.com/2023/05/01/most-important-skills-employers-want

25. https://workforceinstitute.org/wp-content/uploads/2019/11/Full-Report-Generation-Z-in-the-Workplace.pdf

26. "Reskilling Revolution," n.d., https://initiatives.weforum.org/reskilling-revolution/home

27. Stéphane Garelli, "Why You Will Probably Live Longer Than Most Big Companies," IMD Business School for Management and Leadership Courses, December 2016, https://www.imd.org/research-knowledge/disruption/articles/why-you-will-probably-live-longer-than-most-big-companies

28. Austen Gregerson, "Examples of Reskilling and Upskilling Programs," Gloat, April 19, 2024, https://gloat.com/blog/5-successful-examples-of-reskilling-and-upskilling-programs

29. Joseph B. Fuller et al., "Hidden Workers: Untapped Talent," September 2021, https://www.hbs.edu/managing-the-future-of-work/Documents/research/hiddenworkers09032021.pdf

30. Upwork Research Institute, *Work Innovator Report*, November 2, 2023.

31. "Explaining the Growth of the Alternative Workforce," National Bureau of Economic Research, n.d., https://www.nber.org/digest/dec16/explaining-growth-alternative-workforce

31. "Freelance Forward 2023," n.d., https://www.upwork.com/research/freelance-forward-2023-research-report

32. Claudine Bianchi, "What Are 'Middle-skilled' Workers and How Are They Helping Manufacturing Realize Digital Transformation?"

Smart Industry, June 29, 2023, https://www.smartindustry.com/benefits-of-transformation/human-capital/article/33007412/what-are-middle-skilled-workers-and-how-are-they-helping-manufacturing-realize-digital-transformation

34. Manufacturing Institute, "Future Skill Needs in Manufacturing: A Deep Dive," October 2022, https://www.themanufacturinginstitute.org/wp-content/uploads/2022/10/NAM_Rockwell-PTC-Study.pdf

35. Andreas Damelang and Michael Otto, "Who Is Replaced by Robots? Robotization and the Risk of Unemployment for Different Types of Workers," *Work and Occupations*, March 15, 2023, https://doi.org/10.1177/07308884231162953

36. Ian Shine and Kate Whiting, "These Are the Jobs Most Likely to Be Lost – and Created – Because of AI," World Economic Forum, May 4, 2023, https://www.weforum.org/agenda/2023/05/jobs-lost-created-ai-gpt

Chapter 3

1. 75 Intelligence Quotes for Inspiration and Sharing," Indeed, September 30, 2022, https://www.indeed.com/career-advice/career-development/intelligence-quotes

2. Aneesh Raman and Maria Flynn, "When Your Technical Skills Are Eclipsed, Your Humanity Will Matter More Than Ever," *New York Times*, February 14, 2024, https://www.nytimes.com/2024/02/14/opinion/ai-economy-jobs-colleges.html

3. David Autor, "AI Could Actually Help Rebuild the Middle Class," NOEMA, February 12, 2024, https://www.noemamag.com/how-ai-could-help-rebuild-the-middle-class

Chapter 4

1. Tim Marcin, "Ernest Hemingway Quotes: On His Birthday, 14 Memorable Sayings, Photos to Remember Author Born in 1898," *International Business Times*, July 21, 2015, https://www.ibtimes.com/ernest-hemingway-quotes-his-birthday-14-memorable-sayings-photos-remember-author-born-2016518

2. Jordan Turner, "Employees Seek Personal Value and Purpose at Work. Be Prepared to Deliver," March 29, 2023, https://www.gartner.com/en/articles/employees-seek-personal-value-and-purpose-at-work-be-prepared-to-deliver

3. Stephanie Dhue and Sharon Epperson, "Most Workers Want Their Employer to Share Their Values – 56% Won't Even Consider a Workplace That Doesn't, Survey Finds," CNBC, July 6, 2022, https://www.cnbc

.com/2022/07/01/most-workers-want-their-employer-to-share-their-values.html

4. Jake Herway, "To Get Your People's Best Performance, Start With Purpose," May 21, 2021, https://www.gallup.com/workplace/350060/people-best-performance-start-purpose.aspx

5. https://www.gallup.com/workplace/350060/people-best-performance-start-purpose.aspx

6. Kerry Caufield, "Chevron CEO on Modern Leadership: You Can't Be Afraid to Make Yourself Heard," CNBC, March 3, 2021, https://www.cnbc.com/2021/02/25/chevron-ceo-mike-wirth-on-modern-leadership-make-yourself-heard.html

7. Chevron, "The Chevron Way," http://chevron.com, n.d., https://www.chevron.com/who-we-are/culture/the-chevron-way

8. Caufield, "Chevron CEO on Modern Leadership."

9. Chevron, "The Chevron Way."

10. https://www.nytimes.com/2022/09/14/climate/patagonia-climate-philanthropy-chouinard.html

11. Veronika Sonsev, "Patagonia's Focus on Its Brand Purpose Is Great for Business," *Forbes*, February 20, 2024, https://www.forbes.com/sites/veronikasonsev/2019/11/27/patagonias-focus-on-its-brand-purpose-is-great-for-business/?sh=4c9b607954cb

12. Kenji Explains, "'Don't Buy This Jacket' – Patagonia's Daring Campaign," Medium, November 15, 2022, https://bettermarketing.pub/dont-buy-this-jacket-patagonia-s-daring-campaign-2b37e145046b

13. Sonsev, "Patagonia's Focus on Its Brand Purpose Is Great for Business."

14. "Patagonia Shows How Turning a Profit Doesn't Have to Cost the Earth," McKinsey & Company, April 20, 2023, https://www.mckinsey.com/industries/agriculture/our-insights/patagonia-shows-how-turning-a-profit-doesnt-have-to-cost-the-earth

15. Yvon Chouinard, *Let My People Go Surfing: The Education of a Reluctant Businessman*, 2005, http://ci.nii.ac.jp/ncid/BB14724983

16. https://www.inc.com/scott-mautz/how-can-patagonia-have-only-4-percent-worker-turnover-hint-they-pay-activist-employees-bail.html

17. Chouinard, *Let My People Go Surfing*.

18. https://www.forbes.com/sites/veronikasonsev/2019/11/27/patagonias-focus-on-its-brand-purpose-is-great-for-business/?sh=84d676454cb8

19. Yume Murphy, "Blackout Tuesday 2020: One Year Later, What Have Companies Done for Black Lives?" Vox, June 2, 2021, https://www.vox.com/the-goods/22463723/blackout-tuesday-blm-sephora-starbucks-nike-glossier

20. "Most Americans expect brands to take stand on racism," Consulting.us, June 11, 2020, https://www.consulting.us/news/4350/most-americans-expect-brands-to-take-stand-on-racism

21. Murphy, "Blackout Tuesday 2020."

22. Ibid.

23. Marty Johnson, "Mastercard to invest $500 million into Black communities over the next 5 years," The Hill, September 17, 2020, https://thehill.com/policy/finance/516863-mastercard-to-invest-500-million-into-black-communities-over-the-next-5-years

24. Mastercard, "In Solidarity: Standing Against Racism and Advancing Equal Opportunity for All," Mastercard Newsroom, June 25, 2020, https://www.mastercard.com/news/perspectives/2020/in-solidarity-standing-against-racism-and-advancing-equal-opportunity-for-all

25. Cari Nazeer, "What Human-Resources Leaders Are Focusing on Post-Roe," Time, July 12, 2022, https://time.com/charter/6195967/human-resources-roe-v-wade

26. "Here are the companies that will cover travel expenses for employee abortions, June 27, 2022, https://www.nytimes.com/2022/06/24/business/abortion-companies-travel-expenses.html

27. Britt Peterson, "What Gen Z Wants in the Workplace," Washington Post, June 21, 2023, https://www.washingtonpost.com/business/2023/06/16/gen-z-employment#

28. Angel Odukoya, "The Changing Generational Values," Imagine, Johns Hopkins University, October 30, 2023, https://imagine.jhu.edu/blog/2022/11/17/the-changing-generational-values

29. https://www.pewresearch.org/social-trends/2023/12/14/the-growth-of-the-older-workforce

30. Naina Dhingra et al., "Help Your Employees Find Purpose – or Watch Them Leave," McKinsey & Company, April 5, 2021, https://www.mckinsey.com/capabilities/people-and-organizational-performance/our-insights/help-your-employees-find-purpose-or-watch-them-leave

31. https://www.jnj.com/our-credo

32. Tom Bergeron, "Why Johnson & Johnson's Famous Credo, Written 80 Years Ago, Is as Impactful Now as Ever," ROI-NJ, December 19, 2023, https://www.roi-nj.com/2023/12/18/healthcare/why-johnson-johnsons-famous-credo-written-80-years-ago-is-as-impactful-now-as-

33. https://www.jnj.com/our-credo

34. Bergeron, "Why Johnson & Johnson's Famous Credo."

Chapter 5

1. Abby, W. (2019). Wolfpack: How to Come Together, Unleash Our Power, and Change the Game. New York: Celadon Books.

2. Yves Van Durme, "Harnessing Worker Agency," Deloitte, January 8, 2023, https://www.deloitte.com/global/en/our-thinking/insights/topics/talent/human-capital-trends/2023/fostering-employee-empowerment.html

3. David Rock and Christy Pruitt-Haynes, "Why Mandates Make Us Feel Threatened," *Harvard Business Review*, September 23, 2021, https://hbr.org/2021/09/why-mandates-make-us-feel-threatened

4. Holger Reisinger and Dane Fetterer, "Forget Flexibility. Your Employees Want Autonomy," *Harvard Business Review*, October 29, 2021, https://hbr.org/2021/10/forget-flexibility-your-employees-want-autonomy

5. Polly Thompson, "Dell workers can stay remote – but they're not going to get promoted," *Business Insider*, March 16, 2024, https://www.businessinsider.com/dell-remote-workers-promotion-return-office-push-flexible-work-2024-3

6. Nick Paul Taylor, "Sanofi guarantees employees one year of salary and support after cancer diagnosis," *Fierce Pharma*, February 5, 2024, https://www.fiercepharma.com/marketing/sanofi-guarantees-employees-1-year-salary-and-support-after-cancer-diagnosis

7. Michael, L.W. (2020). The importance of self-determination to the quality of life of people with intellectual disability: A perspective. *International Journal of Environmental Research and Public Health* 17 (19): 7121, https://www.ncbi.nlm.nih.gov/pmc/articles/PMC7579126

8. Joanne Stephane, Heather McBride Leef, Sameen Affaf et al., "Uncovering Culture: A Call to Action for Leaders," Deloitte, 2023, https://www2.deloitte.com/content/dam/Deloitte/us/Documents/about-deloitte/dei/us-uncovering-culture-a-call-to-action-for-leaders.pdf?dl=2

9. Emily Field et al., "Women in the Workplace 2023," McKinsey & Company, October 5, 2023, https://www.mckinsey.com/featured-insights/diversity-and-inclusion/women-in-the-workplace#

10. Michele Norris, "Opinion: Our True Feelings about Race and Identity Are Revealed in Six Words," *Washington Post*, January 11, 2024, https://www.washingtonpost.com/opinions/interactive/2024/race-identity-michele-norris-hidden-conversations-race-card-project

11. Emily Peck, "The number of striking U.S. workers more than doubled in 2023," *Axios*, February 15, 2024, https://www.axios.com/2024/02/15/strikes-unions-workers-statistics-chart-data

12. Natalie Rose Goldberg, "The Bottom Line: Labor Unions, with Power and Popularity Rising, Are Still Trailing in the Biggest Nationwide Battle," CNBC, January 28, 2024, https://www.cnbc.com/2024/01/28/unions-with-power-popularity-rising-are-still-losing-a-big-battle.html

13. Greg Rosalsky, "You May Have Heard of the 'Union Boom.' The Numbers Tell a Different Story," NPR, February 28, 2023, https://www.npr.org/sections/money/2023/02/28/1159663461/you-may-have-heard-of-the-union-boom-the-numbers-tell-a-different-story

14. Ted Van Green, "Majorities of Adults See Decline of Union Membership as Bad for the U.S. and Working People," Pew Research Center, March 12, 2024, https://www.pewresearch.org/short-reads/2024/03/12/majorities-

of-adults-see-decline-of-union-membership-as-bad-for-the-us-and-working-people

15. Heidi Shierholz, Margaret Poydock, and Celine McNicholas, "Unionization Increased by 200,000 in 2022," Economic Policy Institute, January 19, 2023, https://www.epi.org/publication/unionization-2022

16. Greg Rosalsky, "You May Have Heard of the 'Union Boom.' The Numbers Tell a Different Story," NPR, February 28, 2023, https://www.npr.org/sections/money/2023/02/28/1159663461/you-may-have-heard-of-the-union-boom-the-numbers-tell-a-different-story

17. Steven Greenhouse, "In America, Labor Has an Unusually Long Fuse," *New York Times*, April 4, 2009, https://www.nytimes.com/2009/04/05/weekinreview/05greenhouse.html

18. Zsolt Darvas, "The European Union's Remarkable Growth Performance Relative to the United States," *Bruegel*, October 26, 2023, https://www.bruegel.org/analysis/european-unions-remarkable-growth-performance-relative-united-states

19. Kerry Close, "Real Reason the French Work Less Than Americans Do," *Time*, January 3, 2017, https://time.com/4620759/european-american-work-life-balance

20. Cassie Robertson, Trudy Rebert, and Lynn Rhinehart, "How Companies Benefit When They Support Their Workers by Respecting Worker Choice," U.S. Department of Labor Blog, February 24, 2023, https://blog.dol.gov/2023/02/24/how-companies-benefit-when-they-support-their-workers-by-respecting-worker-choice

21. Lydia Saad, "More in U.S. See Unions Strengthening and Want It That Way," Gallup, August 30, 2023, https://news.gallup.com/poll/510281/unions-strengthening.aspx

22. "Google Employees Write an Open Letter to CEO Sundar Pichai," *Economic Times*, last updated March 23, 2023, https://economictimes.indiatimes.com/news/new-updates/google-employees-write-an-open-letter-to-ceo-sundar-pichai-see-details/articleshow/98948897.cms?from=mdr

23. Will Knight and Steven Levy, "OpenAI Staff Threaten to Quit Unless Board Resigns," *Wired*, November 20, 2023, https://www.wired.com/story/openai-staff-walk-protest-sam-altman

24. Angela Watercutter, "The Hollywood Strikes Stopped AI from Taking Your Job. But for How Long?" *Wired*, December 25, 2023, https://www.wired.com/story/hollywood-saved-your-job-from-ai-2023-will-it-last

25. Tammy Lytle, "How Companies Benefit from Partnering with Unions," *SHRM*, September 7, 2022, https://www.shrm.org/topics-tools/news/hr-magazine/how-companies-benefit-partnering-unions

26. Asha Banerjee, Margaret Poydock, Celine McNicholas et al., "Unions are not only good for workers, they're good for communities and for democracy," Economic Policy Institute, December 15, 2021, https://www.epi.org/publication/unions-and-well-being

27. Egill Bjarnason, "Women across Iceland, including the prime minister, go on strike for equal pay and no more violence," *AP News*, October 25, 2023, https://apnews.com/article/iceland-women-strike-equal-pay-970669466116a2b1a5673a8737089d46

28. United Nations Research Institute for Social Development (UNRISD), "250 years needed to bridge the pay gap," *UNRIC*, September 17, 2020, https://unric.org/en/250-years-needed-to-bridge-the-pay-gap

29. Eva Epker, "Women Handle 75%+ of All Unpaid Labor. Their Health Pays the Price," *Forbes*, October 31, 2023, https://www.forbes.com/sites/evaepker/2023/10/31/women-handle-75-of-all-unpaid-labor-their-health-pays-the-price/?sh=280871b87f91

30. Holly Corbett, "The #MeToo Movement Six Years Later: What's Changed And What's Next," *Forbes*, November 16, 2023, https://www.forbes.com/sites/hollycorbett/2023/11/16/the-metoo-movement-six-years-later-whats-changed-and-whats-next

31. Kim Elsesser, "Congress Passes Law Restoring Victims' Voices, Banning NDAs In Sexual Harassment Cases," *Forbes*, November 16, 2022, https://www.forbes.com/sites/kimelsesser/2022/11/16/congress-passes-law-restoring-victims-voices-banning-ndas-in-sexual-harassment-cases

32. Becca Damante, Lauren Hoffman, and Rose Khattar, "Quick Facts About State Salary Range Transparency Laws," CAP 20, March 9, 2023, https://www.americanprogress.org/article/quick-facts-about-state-salary-range-transparency-laws/#:~:text=8%20states%20have%20enacted%2C%20and,considering%2C%20salary%20range%20transparency%20laws&text=Map%20showing%20the%20states%20that,%2C%20Rhode%20Island%2C%20and%20Washington

33. Megan Cerullo, "New York pay transparency law drives change in job postings across U.S.," CBS News, September 21, 2023, https://www.cbsnews.com/news/new-york-pay-transparency-law-job-postings

34. Amy McCaig, "Businesses Backing #BlackLivesMatter Are More Attractive to Workers, Have Better Bottom Lines," Rice University News and Media Relations Office of Public Affairs, November 16, 2022, https://news.rice.edu/news/2022/businesses-backing-blacklivesmatter-are-more-attractive-workers-have-better-bottom-lines

35. D. O'Boyle, "5 Ways to Make the Most of Employee Voice," Gallup, November 3, 2023, https://www.gallup.com/workplace/513554/ways-employee-voice.aspx

36. Russ Lidstone, "Associate and Emanate: Five Steps to Improving Employee Engagement," *Forbes*, March 31, 2023, https://www.forbes.com/sites/forbesbusinesscouncil/2023/03/31/associate-and-emanate-five-steps-to-improving-employee-engagement/?sh=3d5d7ca83571

Chapter 6

1. Herb Scribner, "21 Quotes from Arianna Huffington about Sleep and Mental Health from the Qualtrics X4 Summit," *Deseret News*, March 7, 2018, https://www.deseret.com/2018/3/7/20641259/21-quotes-from-arianna-huffington-about-sleep-and-mental-health-from-the-qualtrics-x4-summit

2. World Health Organization, "Burn-out an 'occupational phenomenon,'" International Classification of Diseases, 11th revision, *World Health Organization*, May 28, 2019, https://www.who.int/standards/classifications/frequently-asked-questions/burn-out-an-occupational-phenomenon

3. Jonathan Malesic, "Burnout Dominated 2021. Here's the History of Our Burnout Problem," *Washington Post*, January 1, 2022, https://www.washingtonpost.com/history/2022/01/01/burnout-history-freudensberger-maslach

4. Tracy Brower, "Managers Have Major Impact on Mental Health: How to Lead for Wellbeing," *Forbes*, January 29, 2023, https://www.forbes.com/sites/tracybrower/2023/01/29/managers-have-major-impact-on-mental-health-how-to-lead-for-wellbeing/?sh=365a3e2a2ec1

5. Abby McCain, "22 Telling Employee Wellness Statistics [2023]: How Many Companies Have Wellness Programs," Zippia, November 14, 2022, https://www.zippia.com/advice/employee-wellness-statistics

6. Leonard L. Berry, Ann M. Mirabito, and William B. Baun, "What's the Hard Return on Employee Wellness Programs?" *Harvard Business Review*, December 2010, https://hbr.org/2010/12/whats-the-hard-return-on-employee-wellness-programs

7. Connie Chen, "There Is a Tangible ROI for Businesses That Invest in Mental Health," *Forbes*, October 10, 2023, https://www.forbes.com/sites/forbesbusinesscouncil/2023/10/10/there-is-a-tangible-roi-for-businesses-that-invest-in-mental-health/?sh=779439733b53

8. "Employee Wellbeing Is Key for Workplace Productivity," *Gallup*, https://www.gallup.com/workplace/215924/well-being.aspx

9. Anxiety Skyrockets as Number One Presenting Issue Among American Workers Seeking Mental Health Assistance, ComPsych, March 26, 2024, https://www.compsych.com/press-room/press-article?nodeId=9ab16c66-0c95-44d5-a455-9962b8e67398&utm_source=Iterable&utm_medium=email&utm_campaign=campaign_9692800

10. Pavithra Mohan, "Etsy and UPS Have Seen an ROI of More than 90% from Childcare Benefits," *Fast Company*, March 26, 2024, https://www.fastcompany.com/91069732/etsy-and-ups-have-seen-an-roi-of-over-90-from-childcare-benefits

11. Jen Fisher and Paul H. Silverglate, "The C-suite's Role in Well-being," Deloitte, June 22, 2022, https://www2.deloitte.com/us/en/insights/topics/leadership/employee-wellness-in-the-corporate-workplace.html

12. Ibid.

13. Jessica Booth and Rachel Adams, "How Maternity Leave Affects Your Health," *Forbes Health*, October 9, 2023, https://www.forbes.com/health/womens-health/how-maternity-leave-affects-health

14. Upwork Research Institute. *Reinventing Work: Unveiling the Work Innovators' Blueprint for Success*, 2023.

15. Jordan Turner, "The Secret to Productive Employees? A Radical Shift in Work Flexibility," Gartner, April 20, 2023, https://www.gartner.com/en/articles/the-secret-to-productive-employees-a-radical-shift-in-work-flexibility

16. Queensland Brain Institute, "Half of World's Population Will Experience a Mental Health Disorder," *Harvard Medical School*, July 31, 2023, https://hms.harvard.edu/news/half-worlds-population-will-experience-mental-health-disorder

17. "The Impacts of Poor Mental Health in Business," BerkeleyExecEd, September 29, 2022, https://executive.berkeley.edu/thought-leadership/blog/impacts-poor-mental-health-business

18. Erica Coe, Jenny Cordina, Kana Enomoto, et al., "National Surveys Reveal Disconnect Between Employees and Employers Around Mental Health Need," McKinsey & Company, April 21, 2021, https://www.mckinsey.com/industries/healthcare/our-insights/national-surveys-reveal-disconnect-between-employees-and-employers-around-mental-health-need

19. Garen Staglin, "Confronting Anxiety About AI: Workplace Strategies for Employee Mental Health," *Forbes*, December 18, 2023, https://www.forbes.com/sites/onemind/2023/12/18/confronting-anxiety-about-ai-workplace-strategies-for-employee-mental-health/?sh=383f3bb61f24

Chapter 7

1. Jaywon Choe and Harry Zahn, "My humanity is caught up in yours: How Desmond Tutu dedicated his life to greater good," PBS, December 27, 2021, https://www.pbs.org/newshour/show/my-humanity-is-caught-up-in-yours-how-desmond-tutu-dedicated-his-life-to-greater-good

2. Katherine Fan, "The other AI is stealing our zest for life, relationship expert Esther Perel tells SXSW," *Austin American Statesman*, March 12, 2023, https://www.statesman.com/story/entertainment/arts/2023/03/12/esther-perel-sxsw-2023-artificial-intimacy-adult-loneliness-relationships/69999354007

3. Mark C. Perna, "Why a lack of human connection is crippling your work culture," *Forbes*, October 24, 2022, https://www.forbes.com/sites/markcperna/2022/10/24/why-a-lack-of-human-connection-is-crippling-your-work-culture

4. Priya Parker (2018). *The Art of Gathering: How We Meet and Why It Matters*. New York: Riverhead Books.

5. Mark C. Perna, "Why a Lack of Human Connection Is Crippling Your Work Culture," *Forbes*, October 24, 2022, https://www.forbes .com/sites/markcperna/2022/10/24/why-a-lack-of-human-connection-is-crippling-your-work-culture

6. Kate Murphy, "We're All Socially Awkward Now," *New York Times*, September 1, 2020, https://www.nytimes.com/2020/09/01/sunday-review/coronavirus-socially-awkward.html

7. "Workplace Woes: Meetings Edition," Work Life by Atlassian, https://www.atlassian.com/blog/workplace-woes-meetings

8. Kelli María Korducki, "Research Confirms the Importance of Healthy Workplace Relationships," Atlassian, August 11, 2023, https://www.atlassian .com/blog/teamwork/importance-of-healthy-workplace-relationships

9. Ibid.

Chapter 8

1. Horace Dediu, "Steve Jobs' Ultimate Lesson for Companies," *Harvard Business Review*, August 25, 2011, https://hbr.org/2011/08/steve-jobss-ultimate-lesson-fo

2. https://hbr.org/2011/08/steve-jobss-ultimate-lesson-fo

3. Robert M. Solow, "We'd Better Watch Out," *New York Times Book Review*, July 12, 1987, http://www.standupeconomist.com/pdf/misc/solow-computer-productivity.pdf

4. Sarah Lynch, "A.I. Could Replace CEOs – and They Know It," *Inc.*, September 19, 2023, https://www.inc.com/sarah-lynch-/ai-could-replace-ceos-they-know-it.html

5. Asana, "The State of Collaboration Technology: Research-Backed Strategies for Decoding Digital Clutter and Resetting Your Tech Stack," December 2023, https://asana.com/work-innovation-lab/wp-content/uploads/2023/12/The-State-of-Collaboration-Technology-Research-Backed-Strategies-for-Decoding-Digital-Clutter-and-Resetting-Your-Tech-Stack_121223.pdf

6. "Potential Project Latest Research," Potential Project, https://assets-global .website-files.com/5ff86e096165bce79acc825c/6582bae7f92ec39e160cf 78c_PP-Graph-AI-01-%20OnePage.pdf

7. Paige McGlauflin and Emma Burleigh, "Gen Z Workers Think Their Employers Don't Care About Their Career Growth, So They're Turning to ChatGPT for Job Advice," *Fortune*, February 13, 2024, https://fortune .com/2024/02/13/gen-z-using-ai-tools-for-career-advice-chatgpt

8. Alan Murray, CEO Daily Email, *Fortune*, retrieved on February 15, 2024.

9. Udemy Business, "2022 Workplace Learning Trends Report," 2022, https://info.udemy.com/rs/273-CKQ-053/images/2022_Workplace_LearningTrends_Report.pdf

10. Paychex WORX Blog, "Employees Weigh In on What's Important to Them and Why They Stay at Their Companies," Paychex, July 28, 2022, https://www.paychex.com/articles/human-resources/employee-retention-what-makes-employees-stay-leave

11. Daniel Kurt, "Corporate Leadership by Race," Investopedia, February 15, 2024, https://www.investopedia.com/corporate-leadership-by-race-5114494

12. Gemma Joyce, "Five Times Customers Asked for Change and Brands Actually Delivered It," *Brandwatch*, July 12, 2018, https://www.brandwatch.com/blog/5-times-customer-change

13. "The Link Between Glassdoor Reviews & Customer Satisfaction," Glassdoor for Employers, n.d., https://www.glassdoor.com/employers/resources/link-between-glassdoor-reviews-customer-satisfaction

14. Noam Scheiber, "How Uber Uses Psychological Tricks to Push Its Drivers' Buttons," *New York Times*, April 2, 2017, https://www.nytimes.com/interactive/2017/04/02/technology/uber-drivers-psychological-tricks.html

15. Mike Isaac, "Travis Kalanick, Uber Chief, Apologizes After Fight with Driver," *New York Times*, March 1, 2017, https://www.nytimes.com/2017/03/01/technology/uber-chief-apologizes-after-video-shows-him-arguing-with-driver.html

16. Noah Kirsch, "The Inside Story of Papa John's Toxic Culture," *Forbes*, July 19, 2018, https://www.forbes.com/sites/forbesdigitalcovers/2018/07/19/the-inside-story-of-papa-johns-toxic-culture/?sh=25e4ebd83019

17. Marwa Eltagouri, "Papa John's Founder Will Step Down as CEO after Criticizing National Anthem Protests in the NFL," *Washington Post*, December 21, 2017, https://www.washingtonpost.com/news/business/wp/2017/12/21/papa-johns-founder-replaced-as-ceo-weeks-after-blaming-the-nfl-for-sagging-pizza-sales

18. Jen Colletta, "Inside the DE&I-Focused Culture Transformation at Papa John's," HRExecutive, November 17, 2022, https://hrexecutive.com/inside-the-dei-focused-culture-transformation-at-papa-johns

19. https://www.vice.com/en/article/gorillas-delivery-app-fires-workers-for-striking/

20. https://techcrunch.com/2022/12/09/instant-grocery-app-getir-acquires-its-competitor-gorillas/

21. Jon Youshaei, "3 Ways to Be a More Transparent Leader," *Forbes*, November 19, 2021, https://www.forbes.com/sites/jonyoushaei/2021/11/19/3-ways-to-be-a-more-transparent-leader

22. Orianna Rosa Royle, "Microsoft CEO Satya Nadella does not see empathy as a soft skill: 'It's the hardest skill we learn,'" *Fortune*, October 18, 2023, https://fortune.com/2023/10/18/microsoft-ceo-satya-nadella-empathy-soft-skill

23. "The Power Paradox: How We Gain and Lose Influence" by Dacher Keltner

Chapter 9

1. Alison Beard, "Life's Work: An Interview with Maya Angelou," *Harvard Business Review*, May 2013, https://hbr.org/2013/05/maya-angelou
2. Elizabeth Sawin, "X post," April 26, 2024, https://twitter.com/bethsawin/status/1783837058651582595
3. To learn more about the Theory of Reasoned Action, see Martin Fishbein and Icek Ajzen, *Belief, Attitude, Intention, and Behavior: An Introduction to Theory and Research* (Reading, MA: Addison-Wesley, 1975).
4. A. Chughtai, M. Byrne, and J.F. Barbara, "Linking ethical leadership to employee well-being: The role of trust in supervisor," *Journal of Business Ethics* 127 no. 3 (May 1, 2015): 591–602.
5. Feifan Yang et al., "Leader self-sacrifice: A systematic review of two decades of research and an agenda for future research," *Applied Psychology*, May 18, 2022, https://iaap-journals.onlinelibrary.wiley.com/doi/10.1111/apps.12407
6. Miranda Green, "Office politics is not optional: Learn to play the game or you'll be its victim," *Financial Times*, January 21, 2024, https://www.ft.com/content/a84327c6-f939-480c-925d-19d3f41062bf
7. Sunnie Giles, "The Most Important Leadership Competencies, According to Leaders Around the World," *Harvard Business Review*, March 15, 2016, https://hbr.org/2016/03/the-most-important-leadership-competencies-according-to-leaders-around-the-world
8. Ellyn Shook, "Organizational culture: From always connected to omni-connected," Accenture, 2022, http://www.accenture.com/us-en/insights/strategy/organizational-culture
9. Isaacson, Walter, *Steve Jobs* (New York Simon & Schuster, 2011).
10. Pamela N. Danziger, "Today at Apple: How Angela Ahrendts Imagined a New Apple Retail Experience," Forbes, May 20, 2017, https://www.forbes.com/sites/pamdanziger/2017/05/20/today-at-apple-how-angela-ahrendts-imagined-a-new-apple-retail-experience/?sh=41c60af416eb
11. Scott Davis, "Burberry's Blurred Lines: The Integrated Customer Experience," *Forbes*, July 17, 2014, https://www.forbes.com/sites/scottdavis/2014/03/27/burberrys-blurred-lines-the-integrated-customer-experience/?sh=3c8e986e3cc6
12. Jeff Chu, "Can Apple's Angela Ahrendts Spark a Retail Revolution," Fast Company, January 6, 2014, https://www.fastcompany.com/3023591/angela-ahrendts-a-new-season-at-apple
13. M. Javidan and J. Walker, "A Whole New Global Mindset for Leadership," *People + Strategy* 35, no. 2 (January 2012), https://www.researchgate.net/publication/288959604_A_whole_new_global_mindset_for_leadership

14. Chris Musser, "One Employee Question That Leaders Can't Afford to Ignore," Gallup.Com, September 27, 2019, https://www.gallup.com/workplace/267014/one-employee-question-leaders-afford-ignore.aspx

15. Lynda Gratton, "How to Do Hybrid Right," *Harvard Business Review*, January 19, 2023, https://hbr.org/2021/05/how-to-do-hybrid-right

Acknowledgments

Thank you to the leaders in our lives who have been powerful examples of emotional maturity and human-led leadership: Charles J. Smith Jr., Jenny Myers, Diana O'Brien, Kaye Foster, Kim Davis, Mike Wirth, the MAKERS Circle women, Melissa Waters, and Hayden Brown. The lessons you have taught us along the way gave us the courage and conviction to write this book.

Thank you to all of our colleagues who have supported us on this journey. The gift of these friendships with clients, mentors, and mentees have uplifted and motivated us to draw greater attention to the urgent need for a reinvention of leadership.

A huge thank-you to Jesse Wiley for your sponsorship and belief in us and this book. We have deep gratitude for our editorial team: Zachary Schisgal, Amanda Payne, Michelle Hacker, Sunnye Collins, and Amy Handy. To our extended team at Book Highlights, Mat Miller, Peter Knox, Brian Morrison, Alana Whitman, and Margaret Wiggins, a huge thanks. And to Anne Smith, thank you for lending us your expertise and invaluable insights.

To our spouses and families, thank you for your support, enthusiasm, love, and patience. We hope we have made you proud and that this book is an expression of our values and commitment to make the world a better place. This book is possible because of our love for one another.

Finally, to Julie Myers, our rock, co-conspirator, sage, muse, and so much more. Julie, this book would not have been possible without you and all your gifts. You have inspired us to be better and do better as leaders, authors, and friends. Your influence is in every word of this book. We love you, and there are simply no words to express our gratitude.

About the Authors

CHRISTIE SMITH, PhD

Dr. Christie Smith has over 35 years of experience advising the C-Suite of Fortune 500 companies. She has held global leadership positions at Deloitte, Apple, and Accenture as a highly respected expert in leadership, talent management, organizational design, workforce management, change management, and executive team performance. Christie led the Global Talent & Organization consulting practice at Accenture. As Managing Principal of Deloitte Consulting, she was responsible for the West Region Consulting practice and the development of the Deloitte University Centers for Inclusion and Community Impact. Her leadership in Inclusion and Diversity at Apple was integral to the growth, development, and representation of female and underrepresented groups internally as well as in product and retail solutions. She is a highly sought-after speaker on business strategy, leadership and culture, DEI, people analytics, and the impact of workforce technologies and AI. Her work has been featured in the *New York Times*, the *Wall Street Journal, Harvard Business Review, Fortune, Forbes*, and CNN. Christie has been recognized as a Top 50 Diversity Leader and in Fast Company's Queer 50 list. She is the founder of The Humanity Studio™, a research and advisory institute dedicated to improving the way we live by revolutionizing the way we work. Christie received her doctorate in clinical social work with a focus on leadership and culture from New York University.

KELLY MONAHAN, PhD

Dr. Kelly Monahan is a researcher and managing director of the Upwork Research Institute. With the mission to change work, one insight at a time, the institute's current focus is on unlocking greater productivity and connection in distributed work models, AI's impact on the workforce, and organizational culture change. Kelly's research has been recognized and published in both applied and academic journals, including *MIT Sloan Management Review*, *Harvard Business Review*, and the *Journal of Strategic Management*. Her work has also been featured in publications such as *Fortune*, *Forbes*, and *Business Insider*. In 2018, Kelly released her first book, *How Behavioral Economics Influences Management Decision-Making: A New Paradigm* (Academic Press/Elsevier Publishers). Kelly is a sought-after speaker on how to apply new management and talent models in knowledge-based organizations and is frequently quoted in the media on talent decision-making and the future of work. In 2019, she gave her first TedX Talk on the future of work. Dr. Monahan holds a PhD in organizational leadership from Regent University.

Index

185